,ʃɪ ʃɪʃ   **DATE DUE**

Positive
Thinking,
Positive
Action

Positive Thinking, Positive Action

ESSENTIAL STEPS TO ACHIEVE YOUR POTENTIAL

DOUGLAS MILLER

Published by BBC Worldwide Learning, BBC Worldwide Limited,
Woodlands, 80 Wood Lane, London W12 0TT

First published 2005. Copyright © Douglas Miller 2005
The moral right of the author has been asserted.

ISBN: 0 563 51940 1

Commissioning Editor: Emma Shackleton
Project Editor: Patricia Burgess
Copy Editor: Christine King
Designer: Annette Peppis
Production Controller: Man Fai Lau

Set in Frutiger
Printed and bound in Great Britain by Mackays of Chatham

Contents

Note for the reader   7

Introduction   8

Chapter 1 **We can all be extraordinary**   22

Chapter 2 **Travelling to other worlds**   42

Chapter 3 **Feeding the fire**   58

Chapter 4 **Tuning in**   84

Chapter 5 **Go where you want to go**   96

Chapter 6 **Oxygenation – getting the freshness back!**   120

Chapter 7 **Playing for a living**   144

Chapter 8 **Controlling the heat**   172

Personal resources   181

References   191

Acknowledgements   192

Note for the reader

I have chosen to refer to myself as 'we' throughout this book, unless I am referring directly to a personal experience or my specific suggestions for exercises and so on. The reason is that while this book is a personal 'take' on the subject of positive thinking and positive action, all my thoughts, feelings and perspectives have come from my interactions with the world and the people in it – so it seems right to refer to 'we'. I also refer to you, the reader, not only as 'you' where appropriate, but also as part of the 'we'. The 'we' is the family of positive thinkers, and you are very welcome to join us. By picking up this book, you have already done something positive.

The greater part of our happiness or misery depends upon our dispositions, and not upon our circumstances.

Martha Washington, wife of US president George Washington

Introduction

❑ What is positive thinking?

❑ What can positive thinking do for me?

❑ When can I start to be positive?

❑ The three Rs

❑ Where to now?

■ What is positive thinking?

The term 'positive thinking' was first popularized by inspirational American writer Norman Vincent Peale in 1952. Since then, with the surge of interest in personal learning and development, the world has had the benefit of thousands of books on the subject. The words themselves have gone through the full wash cycle: 'positive mental attitude' and the later 'optimal thinking' are just two versions that have become part of the currency of personal growth.

In recent years the subject has been treated like an exact science, almost as though if you put the right ten coins in the slot machine a positive person will come out of the dispenser below. But we are only barely beginning to understand ourselves. We almost burst with complexity and contradiction – to the point where we may never truly understand what makes us tick. If this is a negative-sounding point on which to start a positive-thinking book, it is actually completely the opposite. It is that very complexity that provides us with the explosion of challenge and opportunity, the potential for success or failure, which are a part of life for each of us.

How exciting too that we have this global laboratory of 6 billion personalities with which we can interact. A central point of this book is that it is this interaction with our multiple worlds – our own and those of others – that leads us to truly understand what the world can give us and what we can give it. We can interact with our inner selves. This interaction generates the self-awareness that is nirvana for us as positive thinkers. The 'complexity of me' is a joy, not a burden. That complexity extends to our outer world too.

Making sense of it all

We can often find 'form' in this complexity. We've all seen the kind of 'modern art' that looks as if the artist has just thrown pigment at the canvas rather than actually painting something. Some of us dismiss these paintings as rubbish and move on. Some of us decide to look a bit longer and find some kind of 'form' in all the chaos. We look for things that we can recognize – even if it is our imagination creating the image for us. It can be a bit like that with positive thinking too. If we choose to, amid the complexity that is each unique person, we can find 'form' – things that we can recognize – which begin to paint the canvas that is positive thinking. These are some of the things that we can say with confidence:

■ It's not all in the genes

Some say positive thinking comes as a genetic inheritance. They say, 'We're born that way.' Life could be very tough if we imagine ourselves to be one of those people who believe that they haven't got the right genes. We ask the question: How many babies and very young children do we see being negative? Uncontaminated by life's negative experiences, they feel free to express themselves, to try new things, to have no fear of making mistakes and to act like a sponge for new learning. It's the low points we all encounter in day-to-day living that can eat away at our positive state and turn us into people who lack confidence, who are pessimistic and who think that life happens to them. As we get older, we find it harder to retain that positive vitality we had when we were young. The vitality never leaves us – it just gets suppressed by the flotsam we pick up on life's journey.

■ We all have a fire within ourselves

We are all born with a flame in us – motivation – that burns continuously. Some have a roaring fire and the flames need to be controlled. Others have a flicker that with the application of positive thinking can be turned into something more substantial. But none of us has no flame at all. The evidence? Getting out of bed, cooking a meal, going to work, learning to drive, watching a ball game – all require a level of motivation, no matter how small. We make decisions to do things all the time. The fire was lit at birth.

■ We can choose to add fuel to the fire

Within us lie all the ingredients we need to be positive. Being positive comes more naturally to some than others. Some of us may have to work a bit harder to bring our 'positive self' out into the open – we find ourselves later in life. Readers who need convincing might try logging on to their country's website that gives news of old school friends (for example, Classmates.com in the US, Friends Reunited in the UK). Those you thought were destined for a life of achievement may well have not moved far. Those who perhaps at that earlier stage of life hadn't connected with themselves may have gone on to experience what appear to highly fulfilling, positive vocations. We can only imagine what has happened in between.

■ We need to keep an open mind

There are contradictions, curiosities and changes all around us, and this book is no exception: it holds a mirror up to life. By challenging what it says, we are more likely to understand what positive thinking means to us. For example, it recommends clear goal-setting as a powerful motivating force – however, there are times when the fixed goal will act as a barrier to trying new things. Sometimes just trying new things with our eyes open but with no self-imposed limitation on where we might get to can create opportunities for us that we couldn't envisage. Don't be put off by contradiction. Just keep an open mind.

■ We need to keep a global perspective

The characteristics of positive thinking in one culture will be anathema to another. For example, the 'can do' mentality prevalent in North American and north European cultures – in which it may be seen as a characteristic of positive thinkers – can be regarded as selfish, anti-social behaviour in other cultures. The world seems to be on the verge of a major change as China and India become serious global players, and the influence of those very distinctive cultures on the world will be interesting. One of the characteristics of positive thinkers is that we see a world of 6 billion people and are open-minded enough to absorb and understand the perspectives, opinions and uniqueness that are the worlds of each person.

■ What can positive thinking do for me?

Before reading on, have a go at answering that question for yourself. Think for a moment about the things that have stopped you achieving what you want, and make a list of them.

When we look at the list, we begin to see that many of the things in it are those that we have some level of personal control over – lack of confidence, no real purpose, haven't had the opportunities and so on. These are the things we work with closely in this book: the things in our life over which we have some control. So, to the question 'What can positive thinking do for me?' I'd answer:

■ **Positive thinking** combines optimism, determination, energy and self-belief wrapped up as a present you are able to give to yourself.

■ **Positive thinking** powers an internalized flame that takes you from 'aspiration' to achievement. The more powerful the heater – from a spark through to a raging fire – the more likely the aspiration will be made real.

■ **Positive thinking** delivers you from an ambient state of 'being' to a frame of mind that is 'all-seeing'.

■ **Positive thinking** provides a framework for successful survival and future achievement, no matter what your current circumstances might be.

■ **Positive thinking** helps to create, out of your own imagination, your reality.

Can thinking positively make me successful?

It can be easy to take the words 'positive thinking' and sell only the one-dimensional materialistic benefits. Assuming with some justification that we want to think positively to help us nurture and grow 'success' for ourselves (and in others), the assumption kicks in that this means financial attainment. And for some this works very well. It is interesting that the common phrase 'health, wealth and happiness' places wealth before happiness. Health is important, although, as many studies tell us, happiness, fulfilment and life-enrichment often provide a fundamental building block in the maintenance of good health and/or overcoming illness. But does wealth buy happiness? Maybe. It gets most of us to some sort of base camp. But is it the thing that delivers success for us? Will we define success by the size of our bank account? Do we have to be rich to make our life rich?

> *Life is not worth living if we exercise our profession only for the sake of material success and do not find in our calling an inner necessity and a meaning that transcends the mere earning of money, a meaning which gives our life dignity and strength.*
> Charles Repke, *A Humane Economy: The Social Framework of the Free Market,* quoted in de Graaf et al, *Affluenza*

Does wealth get us to the top of the mountain? Why, when we try to give meaning to the word 'success', do so many of us want to attach the words 'millionaire' or 'successful businessman/woman' to the word to make it resonate? Search 'success' on the internet and we get business people and superstars – a very narrow definition of what constitutes success in our world! There are going to be an awful lot of unsuccessful people out there if that's all there is for us.

Nobody has the right to define what success means for anybody else. What we define as success is a personal decision. Some readers may be uncomfortable with the linking together of 'positive thinking' and 'success', but it is a widely held contention that as human beings we need to feel a purpose in our life, we need to feel we add value to the world, and the word 'success' implies that we have made a contribution – while maintaining, as Charles Repke says, our dignity.

While it is undoubtedly a motivating factor for some of us, the need to 'perform' to a set of criteria laid down by society or family and friends can be restrictive in that we may try to lead the life that others think we (or for that matter they) should be living. We cease to be ourselves. Our success, our personal 'contribution', can only ultimately be defined and judged by our own very personal set of criteria. We are successful when we 'feel' it.

I can tell the reader that success for me will be the point, close to the end of my life, where I feel I have made an impact, a difference, and expressed myself to the world as best I can. I will feel it, but I know I won't be able to measure it.

Your definition will probably be very different. What might success feel like to you?

I am extraordinary!

We are under a lot of pressure to be ordinary. It is an annoying habit of politicians, for example, to refer to 'ordinary people'. We hear the US president say 'ordinary Americans' as though the word 'ordinary' was supposed to resonate with the people. In the UK the appeal of 1990s' British Prime Minister John Major was supposed to be his 'ordinariness'. But whether we agreed with his politics or not, how could we ever define as 'ordinary' a man who got where he did, having been brought up in a state-owned home, who left school with no qualifications and who got rejected as a bus ticket inspector when applying for his first job? Journalists applied the epithet 'ordinary' because they thought we could identify with that. How many us think we are ordinary?

The challenge is to find the areas of life in which we can be extraordinary.

> *We all have the capacity to do extraordinary things, and that makes us extraordinary. The sadness is that in life so few of us find what makes each of us unique and extraordinary.*

Many of us never even try to access the part of us that can do extraordinary things, and yet there are great people managing to do precisely that. It's just that we don't always hear about them. We can take, for example, the champion US cyclist Lance Armstrong and look at the characteristics that got him to where he is. There is of course much to be learnt from his remarkable life experiences. But there is also much to be learnt from the career nurse in a hospital who has loved her job for 35 years, or the charity workers in an impoverished country who get all the personal nourishment they need through the positive approach they have to their life and in particular their work. Or from a husband and wife who give 30 years of their life to providing a home for foster children. Or it might be someone like you, doing a job you like doing and making an impact while you do it. Positive thinking plays an essential role in taking us to our true level of capability – to the point where we make a positive statement about ourselves to the world.

Debrett's *People of Today* is published every year in the UK and lists around 30,000 people whom it sees as Britain's top 'achievers'. It's an interesting coffee-table read but, as we all know, there are so many heroes out there and often we never get to hear about them. Achievement/success is remarkably difficult to qualify, so let's leave it to the AppleMac dictionary!

> **Achieve** – to succeed in doing or gaining something, usually with effort.
> **Succeed** – to manage to do what is planned or attempted: to do well in an activity, making admirable progress or impressive achievements.

The definition of 'succeed' also makes the usual references to 'fame, wealth and power'!

This is not about the Victorian notion of being satisfied with our 'lot'. It's about recognizing how much there is for us in our short life if we think positively about our capabilities, what it is we *really* want from our life and how we might create a fulfilling role for ourselves.

■ When can I start to be positive?

The answer is a simple one: it is never too late or too early to start thinking and acting in a more positive way.

Starting young

A while ago Roger Waters, formerly of rock group Pink Floyd, and the creative engine behind the classic *Dark Side of the Moon* album, was interviewed in a UK newspaper. He talked about his early years and how he'd always been told that his childhood/adolescence was some kind of preparation for 'life' – this mythical thing that was going to happen to him in adulthood.

When he got to his mid twenties he began to realize that if he sat back and waited for his 'life' to begin, it might never start. He was actually living his 'life' and always had been. We can argue that Roger Waters had already achieved much to be proud of, but his rethink inspired him to write *Dark Side of the Moon*. It is still one of the biggest-selling albums ever made.

The theatre of life is not the sofa!

Whether you've heard of Roger Waters or not, or, indeed, whether you like Pink Floyd or not, his story is a simple exercise in one of the core elements in positive thinking. Simply sitting back and watching events go by ('life happens to me') and hoping perhaps that something will 'stick' to us, absolves us from taking responsibility for our own future. It also means that we confine our future to fate. As positive thinkers, we see opportunity all around and we have the curiosity, the energy and the self-belief to be able to chart a future where we begin the process of taking control.

It's really quite simple. If you believe you can make a difference, you probably will. If you don't, then you probably won't.

Third-age thinking

The attributes of positive thinking apply equally to those in or entering the third age of life – usually at retirement. Western societies grossly neglect the contribution third-agers can make – all that knowledge, experience and wisdom internalized because there isn't a societal mechanism in which it can express itself. Much positive-thinking literature assumes readers are positioned in early to middle age, their energies devoted to career or winning things like the New York Marathon. But why should age be a barrier? The third age gives us that precious commodity: time. There is much in this book for the positive-thinking retiree – not least our capacity to maintain curiosity and interest in the world: a characteristic of all positive thinkers regardless of age.

An octogenarian entrant into one of the world's great street marathons recently said that she realized she probably wasn't going to win it, but that within her capability she had her own goals. We do have to acknowledge that health is a key variable at any age. However, we know that those who think positively, who keep curious and who have an optimistic view of the future can thrive whatever their time of life.

■ The three Rs

Just as the three Rs of reading, writing and 'rithmetic are the foundations of traditional education, so the three Rs of positive thinking – responsibility, renewal and reward – provide a strong basis for us to move forward.

Responsibility

Fate gives us a ready excuse for inertia. The belief that fate is the guiding principle in our life means that we let it be just that with the excuse for failure already built in – 'It was in the lap of the gods'. The positive thinker sees the latent energy in beginning something, and in therefore taking personal responsibility for changing our circumstances for the better.

As Sigmund Freud once said, in another context, 'One day, in retrospect, the years of struggle will strike you as the most beautiful period of your life.' It might be hard to see it that way if you are immersed in the struggle at the moment, faced with personal problems, financial difficulties and stress.

We can overcome these things if we take personal responsibility for them. We can overcome them if we tell ourselves we can. Telling ourselves we can acts as the catalyst for the actions we need to undertake to confront the parts of our life that are causing us difficulty.

Renewal

Let's acknowledge, in the words of boxer Frank Bruno as he recovered from a mental breakdown, that 'Life isn't easy – if it was, everyone would be doing it.' Mini-crises, pessimism, stalled goals, ill health, unwanted change, failure and lack of confidence are part of the fabric of modern-day living for many of us. It's not helpful to disregard these perfectly normal elements of the human condition through overblown rhetoric that dismisses or invites us to dismiss negativity in our thinking. As positive thinkers, we have negative thoughts. Blind faith is as dangerous as no faith. Negative thoughts are perfectly normal human reactions and are a healthy part of us.

The key is to recognize that these are often waves to be ridden rather than unnavigable rivers. Some seem to find it easy to get across to the other side of the river. Others meet tough waters along the way and need all the knowledge and skills they possess to get to the other side. If, like most of us, you fall into the latter camp, a whole range of negativity-inducing things are likely to happen to you through your life. Our feelings of negativity shouldn't be suppressed – channelled in the right way, initial negative feelings can help to generate some much-needed realism. But the negativity shouldn't become all-pervasive to the point where we talk ourselves into inertia.

Even if we've had setback after setback in our life, it's crucial to recognize that we can regenerate ourselves. It is the only option we have. If we are finding it tough at the moment, thinking positively is the best chance we have of taking control.

Reward

In the same way that intuition can lead us up blind alleys if we're not careful, positive thinking can be misappropriated to the point where we convince ourselves to do things because 'I am a positive thinker'. Positive thinkers are decisive. It is often the case that any decision is better than no decision. Don't force it if it doesn't feel right – this is a situation where intuition/gut feeling can be very useful in decision making. On the other hand, don't confuse this feeling with apathy. Nothing can 'feel right' if you choose to wear apathy glasses the whole time.

We can ask, 'What's the pay-off both for me and for others?' And, 'Where might this action take me?' Sometimes we take the action because we are curious about the destination. We have no idea what the destination is but we think it could be good for us – that in itself is a goal because we are consciously feeding our need for novelty and curiosity. Sometimes we do have a clear idea about the end goal – we are very specific about where it is we want to get to: pass the exam, deliver our baby, get promotion, climb the mountain.

▉ Where to now?

Some people believe they can walk on water. Many just want help in getting to the other riverbank. This book aims to be the boat. The boat takes us into Chapter 1 – 'We can all be extraordinary' – where we create our own mini version of Debrett's *People of Today*, featuring four people from around the world who aren't famous but who in their own ways have made an impact on it: people who have decided to access the extraordinary parts of themselves – including one who found fulfilment in the third age of life. All the theory in the world gets us nowhere if we can't see that it can be made real. Our four 'real lives' make it very real!

In Chapter 2 we argue that positive thinking starts with the way we see the world. A world of opportunity, a world where we can express the best parts of our imagination: a world that has 6 billion co-inhabitants in it and the possibilities they create for us. And we must be willing to travel there. In Chapters 3 and 4 we get close to our 'heating system' – the fire within us that gives us the tools we can use to help us think in a more positive way: being optimistic, seizing opportunity, gaining confidence and developing our learning skills.

'There's nothing as practical as a good theory,' said one theorist. The theory of effective goal-setting has occupied many minds. In Chapter 5 we look at the benefits and methods of setting goals for us as positive thinkers – as well as ten suggestions to help you set and reach your own goals.

In Chapter 6 we freshen ourselves up – we 'oxygenate' the mind to keep ourselves vital and alert and the senses in tip-top condition. This chapter helps us do a little 'cranial flossing' – clearing out the 'baggage' of everyday living that builds up over time. We don't need to think about thinking all the time. Take a break!

Chapter 7 brings positive thinking to the workplace as we learn to 'play for a living'. We look at what motivates us at work and how we can get into a mindset that takes us down a rewarding work path. It's estimated that we will spend around 80,000–100,000 hours of our life at work. That's a long time not to be maximizing our enjoyment of it.

The last chapter offers a final check to make sure that positive thinking does not send us down negative – unethical – paths. We can keep the balance here by protecting our integrity and controlling our ego. And ten positive-thinking 'bites' keep us on the positive-thinking road.

A call to action

Reading a book on 'positive thinking' is not an end in itself. It can be tempting to read this book as though it were a novel. We acknowledge the interesting read but treat it as some kind of abstraction from our own world. Our thinking has maybe changed a little when we finish iy, but are we now inclined to act on this changed thinking? The words 'positive thinking' suggest 'thought' – but surely we can choose to take this beyond an interesting read and apply our new thinking practically into the arena of our own life. As futurologist Joel Barker said: 'Vision without action passes the time.' There are therefore lots of practical ideas and exercises to help you apply this thinking in the book. Try them. They will help relate the theory to your own life.

The title of this book – *Positive Thinking: Positive Action* – may suggest that positive thinking in itself is an interesting intellectual exercise, and a necessary start point in creating your action-based environment. We can argue therefore that it is the first action. But the real action comes when you make the thinking real. When you recognize that you can make a contribution, however large or small, you will, in the words of psychologist Mark Brown, 'happen to the world'.

The only person who *has* to believe in you…**is you**.

Chapter 1
We can all be extraordinary

- ❏ Sergio – The skills of the survivor

- ❏ Kath – 'I believe you can do anything'

- ❏ Helene – Third-age thinking

- ❏ Gavin – Moving mountains

- ❏ Learning from 'real life'

One of the advantages of a greater connection with the world and the people in it – one of the key traits of positive thinkers – is that we can learn from them and apply some of their experiences to our own life. We don't need to copy them. But it can be very helpful to get a feel for how others have used a positive approach to their life to help them overcome hurdles, deal with crises, achieve their goals and maximize their opportunities. In this chapter we meet four very different people who are living four very different lives, and see how thinking in a positive way has helped them.

■ Sergio – The skills of the survivor

Sergio was born in Guadalajara, Mexico, in 1947. Early in his life his father abandoned his mother, a peasant woman with little money to support her family. At that time Mexico was controlled by an oppressive civilian dictatorship. Street gangs took part in guerrilla-style action against the government, and Sergio, motivated by the injustices he saw, soon became part of these gangs. He witnessed friends killed, people go missing and communities destroyed by the heavy-handed regime. As Sergio says himself, he had to learn the skills of making himself anonymous for fear of being targeted. However, he couldn't stay anonymous for ever. But at the same time he had the wherewithal to recognize that he needed to create some kind of meaningful existence for himself.

These formative experiences, on both a family and a community level, bred a desire in Sergio, fuelled in part, he says, by a feeling of guilt for having survived such a tough environment when so many of his friends had died on the streets. Remarkably, amid this brutalizing existence Sergio took a significant mental leap – through education.

The Mexican state education system during the 1960s was spartan: the environment wasn't conducive to learning, and the system suffered from a lack of resources and support from central government. In spite of this, Sergio recognized that at least there was an education system and he saw education as a way of improving his circumstances. Here is a great lesson for positive thinkers. Even if circumstances and available resources are less than ideal, we always have the choice of dismissing opportunity (no matter how small the opportunity) or taking the chance we have. Sergio enrolled in the Colegio de

Mexico in the late 1960s, and from there he went to the USA and read for a master's degree at Johns Hopkins University.

The academic world captured Sergio's imagination. He now divides his life into two very distinct parts. He has continued to work in academic environments and has had over 20 books published. But the activist against injustice has never left him, and he resolved to use peaceful methods to do something about it – a principle he carries with him to this day.

A key part of Sergio's life is that he doesn't see academic work as some kind of abstraction from the real world. It has actually given him the freedom and the intellectual basis (as well as the income) to help highlight injustice and instigate change for the better in Mexico. He does not do this for money.

As Sergio made the move from street gang member to academic and human rights campaigner, he's been able to assess what it is about his thinking, about his life, that has taken him to what he calls the 'feeling of control, of total freedom' that he has now. He has identified five 'skills of the survivor' – a mindset that he believes has got him to his current point, but that can be applied in a multitude of situations.

1 Recognize your own strengths and weaknesses

In the early stages of taking a more positive outlook on life, it can pay to make an honest appraisal – a snapshot – of your own strengths and weaknesses. Sergio probably isn't one of life's natural street revolutionaries, and he realized that his effectiveness in changing Mexican society would be best served through peaceful means. So he looked to the strengths he had in him that would best serve the cause of justice and freedom.

2 Adapt to the environment you find yourself in

At one stage in his life Sergio found himself in prison. At other times he was hiding from the authorities. As he says: 'I found myself adapting to the circumstances I was in.' In prison he took the chance to develop his chess skills. When in hiding, he learnt to stay anonymous but to keep himself positive by thinking about things that gave him pleasure. We have in us the capability to adapt mentally to a quite remarkable degree.

Sergio was keeping away from capture and possible imprisonment. He wasn't able to change his circumstances instantly, but he was able (as we all are) to choose his attitude in those circumstances and adapt accordingly. Tough circumstances call for positive responses.

3 Find things to enjoy

This skill picks up on the previous one, where thinking about pleasant things is part of adapting to difficult circumstances. Sergio looks for simple pleasures around him, things that help him draw breath and maintain perspective. He commented: 'Even in the worst circumstances, you can find ways to enjoy yourself.' It may sound simplistic, but many people in tough situations (concentration camp survivors, for example) have made similar comments – a need to remind ourselves about the things, we enjoy in life. Pleasurable thoughts about people, places and things or about pastimes and hobbies, help us to experience joy and pleasure in adverse circumstances.

These factors can be very important when we strive to achieve big long-term goals. Sergio's struggle to fight the cause of human rights and injustice in Mexico is balanced by his enjoyment of life itself. We can argue that his ability to get the most out of his current circumstances actually strengthens him in his life's work.

Perhaps there is a balance to be struck between our enjoyment of the present and the fulfilment of long-term goals. We can see it in the difference between North American and Mediterranean cultures. North American culture could be said to be very goal-focused; sometimes it seems that people really focused on the future in that culture rarely slow down and draw breath. In Mediterranean cultures the *mañana* mentality may be more prevalent when it comes to planning and long-term aspiration, but people here draw heavily on the enjoyment of simple pleasures, such as food, wine, nature and friendship. Both cultural influences can work for us.

4 Recognize and take your chances

Sergio, with a 'searching' mentality, saw educational opportunities where perhaps others, in similar circumstances, weren't even looking. Opportunity-spotting is home to the positive thinker. It's the first step in recognizing that getting control of the future depends on our actions now. The chances for Sergio in this environment were limited, yet he made the choice and saw that he could continue the fight for justice (but now through peaceful means) and educate himself. In the long term his decision has allowed him to be more effective in his battle to highlight injustice and denial of human rights.

In cosy Western societies we can become opportunity-blind. There is so much opportunity that we can become complacent about it. In 1960s' Mexico opportunities were limited but Sergio saw a chance and took it.

5 Look to the future

Optimists see the latent potential in the word 'future'. Imagine having to hide from the authorities and having to keep yourself anonymous to avoid arrest. What would be going through your mind? For Sergio it was the sense that the future would be better for him. And that maybe his own positive actions were what would make that future better. Sergio's thoughts were, and still are, past-, present- and future-orientated. Injustices in the past and present still motivate him, but his actions are geared to creating a more optimistic and achievement-orientated future both for himself and his wider community.

Putting it all into practice

It was perhaps inevitable that at some time in his life Sergio would seek political office. He has stood for Deputy in the National Assembly – the equivalent of a member of the House of Representatives in the USA or a Member of Parliament in the UK. I asked him how he got on (I have to confess I knew the answer when I asked). Sergio laughed loudly and said, 'I failed miserably.' He has retained perspective in his life – as a social reformer rather than a politician. He laughed at the loss but, with such a rich and fulfilling life, a little failure doesn't really mean much. Dwelling on failure would be counter-productive for a person whose life has been hard at some points but who has the success profile in him in abundance. The flame still burns – the desire to overcome injustice, to protect human rights and to champion democracy in his homeland. Mexico still has problems in this area and there is still work to be done. At the age of 57, Sergio shows no sign of declining energies.

He is now in a position where he can explore the world more. His work in the key areas of his life will continue, but he wants to know more about the world and the people in it and has vowed to spend two months in every year travelling (in the next chapter we look at how it can be important for positive thinkers to be curious about people, places and things). Sergio has his own version of that curiosity now. He often sits in a park, shuts his own life off for a minute and observes. He asks such questions as: 'Why are people doing the things they are doing?' Or 'Why are they doing those things in that way?' He's interested in people – he wants to understand them better. Understanding people better helps him to champion their right to be treated as human beings.

■ Kath – 'I believe you can do anything'

Just imagine. You're sitting at your desk at work, doing your job as a brand manager, and you get an email from a friend. It has information about a TV series where members of the public will be undertaking tough physical challenges in some of the more remote parts of the world. Your friend thinks you might be the right person for it. You don't really give it a second thought but mentally make a note of the closing date for entries.

This is the position Kath was in at the beginning of 2004. On the closing date itself she decided to enter, penned a 100-word summary of why she might be the right person, emailed it and waited. A few days later she was invited to a physical testing where 100 members of the public would be put through their paces and eventually whittled down to eight, each of whom would have a TV programme dedicated to their efforts at physical endurance.

The physical testing consisted of non-stop exercise from 7 a.m. to 7 p.m., with Kath being taken to the limit both physically and mentally. Although a degree of physical fitness was required, and Kath admitted she had done no exercise for six months, her real test was to keep at it over the 12 hours, even though her body was screaming to stop. Imagine doing a 12-km (8-mile) run followed by hours of rowing, orienteering and climbing, then doing another run with a rucksack of sand on your back and you get an idea of what Kath had to undertake. Having decided to enter only at the last moment, what kept her going was realizing that she now desperately wanted to be one of the chosen eight. This could be put down to Kath's competitive instinct, but it would also be true to say that she felt she owed it to herself to give everything in the testing session. You cannot half-commit to something that demanding, and there is little point in going through the motions. At the end of the day the 100 exhausted candidates went their separate ways, waiting to hear if they had been selected.

A few days later Kath got a call. A camera was being sent round, which she had to operate herself, together with an envelope that she had to open in front of the camera. She did, and the envelope revealed that she had been selected as one of the eight. The daunting bit was that she would be joining a team of two Finns and an Irishman, Pasi, Iiro and Noel, who had entered the UKATAK – the toughest winter adventure race going, a 500-km (310-mile) trek in Canada across some of the most challenging terrain in the world. And it would be taking place in nine weeks' time.

Kath's team-mates had all participated in UKATAK before. So the question was: is achievement at the most extreme levels of physical endurance the domain of the top few, or can members of the public leading more conventional lives perform at this elite level too? Kath, and millions of TV viewers, were about to find out.

Kath learnt that in the nine weeks before UKATAK she had to condition herself in three disciplines that she had never done before – biking, cross-country skiing and snowshoeing – as these would be how the team would travel. She had to undergo an initial psychological and physical testing to show up weaknesses and strengths. A large part of our success or failure in anything comes from the conversation we have with ourselves about what we are undertaking. With this in mind, and having established that Kath really wanted to do UKATAK, a psychologist asked her, 'Why?' She came up with the following responses:

- Fun.
- Exciting.
- Makes me feel like being alive.
- Proving you can do anything.
- I can do anything!

As one of her coaches so rightly observed, saying 'I can do anything' – and believing it – is a remarkable statement to take through life. It would be something she would need to tell herself regularly through the race itself; particularly in the darkest moments, positive thoughts are what pull us through. The coach worked with Kath to make it clear that she understood what she would be going through psychologically.

On the physical side, Kath's strengths and weaknesses in the three disciplines were tested. It became apparent that she would be weak in the biking section and that she would need to put in a lot of work in this area to get up to scratch – biking requires the use of muscles that are not often used in other sports disciplines. This means that what seems a rather simple discipline – riding a bike – is actually very tough if you plan to bike long distances.

In order to succeed, we do need to be honest about our weaknesses. Being honest about weaknesses ('know yourself') is the first step in overcoming them, and Kath recognized the need to work particularly hard at her biking.

In Chapter 5 we talk about the importance of setting milestones to help us gauge our level of progress in reaching our goals. One of Kath's coaches decided to enter her for the British Cross-country Skiing Championships after only three weeks' practice. As her coach said, at this stage it was important to put a challenge in front of Kath to really channel her thinking.

So how did Kath do? Well, she didn't win it! But after only three weeks' training she managed to beat one other person and finish only two minutes behind two others. She learnt that she was making good progress but hard work lay ahead. Even a tiny success, like in Kath's case beating someone, helped build her belief that she could compete in UKATAK. Says Kath: 'I was a bit unsure about taking part because I had had so little practice, but I was close enough to my competitors to realize I was going in the right direction.'

Kath still had much work to do on her biking skills. She could get help in the race itself because she could get a bike tow off one of her team-mates, but this would slow down the team-mate who was towing her.

A few days before the race, Kath met her team-mates and they began to talk through how they would work as a team during the race. She learnt even more about the thoroughness of preparation required. They were to spend a night out in the open before the race and they were to take their tents with them. Kath thought this would be so they could get some sleep. She was told that they were taking their tents with them so that they could practise putting the tent up when deprived of sleep! She discovered the need to generate realism. Her coaches still weren't convinced that she was sure what she was letting herself in for. Her team-mates left her in no doubt. Five days' racing, with only four hours' sleep across those five days, through the hardest terrain imaginable, sharing sleeping bags (to save carrying extra weight) and utilizing skills she had only just begun to learn, were going to test Kath's mental resolve to the extreme.

And so the race itself began.

The low points...

We often learn just what our bodies and our minds are capable of only when we push them to extremes. Disaster struck Kath on day three when she got a fairly serious hip injury, which might have prevented her finishing. She had to carry on through the pain, helped by her own positive mentality and a supply of painkillers. There is a point where physical pain ceases to become the issue and the mind takes over. As Kath says: 'Your body can go way beyond what you can imagine it is capable of if your mind tells itself it can.' There were times where the pain was bearable and times where she questioned if she could go on. She says: 'I knew it wasn't for ever, that I was nearer the end than the beginning, and that things were going to get better.'

The team had to pick themselves up from a disaster (in the context of the race) even on the first day, when Noel's bike-chain broke. Race rules state that you can only repair equipment, not replace it. Noel was the person most likely to tow Kath up the most challenging hills, so she was now having to rely on her own reserves in her weakest discipline. Recognizing that we have a choice of responses in tough situations takes us a step on the way to choosing a positive one. With a hip injury, and no longer able to be towed as much as before, Kath had to respond positively. As she herself said: 'I was thinking about the team and the people back home who I was competing for [Kath was being sponsored]. I didn't want to let others down.' She responded in the best way possible.

The rollercoaster

As the race wore on, Kath began to experience more and more what she now calls 'the rollercoaster'. She had to tell herself in the dips that 'it is going to get better' and that the end goal was always in sight. As she says herself, 'You have to believe that you will get there.' She also learnt to make the most of the ups. There were times, even when she was beginning to question her capacity to finish, when she found herself getting 'first wind, second wind, third wind...' through the five days. Kath realized that she had to keep talking to herself: 'You have to tell yourself that no matter how bad it gets, there is a point when things get better.' This positive conversation with yourself is crucial.

The team was surviving on as little as 40 minutes' sleep a night. This deprivation can alter your judgement and you can begin to feel as if you are operating in a kind of dream world. Says Kath: 'It's true that you start to imagine things like beds and warmth, but I found that even on 40 minutes' sleep a night, I was able to refresh myself for the next stage of the race.'

And so they came to the last day. Competing against 11 other teams of four people in an alpine wilderness, it's hard to know how you are doing. News came through that, remarkably, they were actually winning! But with only 40 minutes in hand over the second-placed team and with a broken bike and now three of the team injured, it was likely to be a very tough last day. Perhaps in those circumstances it can help to recognize that you are not the only ones going through the pain. In the microcosm of the race the other teams were finding it just as tough. But the possibility of winning pushed Kath and her team-mates on even through the physical problems they were now experiencing.

At the beginning of the race one of the experts had suggested that it would be remarkable if Kath finished the race. He hadn't considered the possibility that she and her team-mates might actually win it! And win it they did. With just nine weeks' notice, little experience in the skills required and virtually no sleep for the five days of the event, Kath was part of the team that won the toughest alpine race in the world.

So what did UKATAK do for Kath? The final words are left to Kath herself:

The whole UKATAK experience has completely captured my imagination. I have so many thoughts, ambitions, ideas coming from it, from climbing Everest, to actually thinking about trying to get to the Olympics, to joining the army, to sailing round the world. All sorts of crazy plans!

My passion for personal adventure is equally matched by my passion for developing people into the best they can be, which I truly believe has so much to do with the mind. I really do believe that anything is possible.

Try something new and who knows where it may take you. Perhaps we will be seeing Kath in a future Olympic Games.

There is a postscript to Kath's story. While she had been preparing for and participating in the UKATAK, her mother was dying of cancer – thoughts of her were very much in Kath's mind as she competed. Even though close to death, Kath's mother was able to see the film of her daughter taking part in and winning the toughest race imaginable. She died just a few days later.

■ Helene – Third-age thinking

Born in 1932 in Vienna, Helene fled to England with her parents from Nazi persecution of Jews in the late 1930s. As she was very young at the time, these experiences play little part in her story. She had a comfortable upbring-ing in England, although, perhaps because of the influence of her parents – who after their experiences rather withdrew into themselves – she found her-self distinctly lacking in confidence. That was until the age of 19, when an opportunity presented itself. She was attending a lecture at college when the class was asked if any of them wanted to go on a special programme with a Freudian psychoanalyst. Only three volunteered for what turned out to be a life-enhancing experience.

Says Helene: 'I had always believed I was an introverted, shy person and because I believed it I behaved like it. In that year I learnt to express my extro-vert side. I managed to unlock and let free the real me!' She learnt in a year what it takes many a lifetime to do. She emerged a more confident, positive, proactive person. 'Something happened to me there. It took a lot for me to make the decision, and I'm still not sure why I did. It was one of two seminal moments of my life.' (The other comes later.) She continues: 'It taught me, something I still believe, that part of being positive is to make a realistic evalu-ation of yourself. I found this extrovert side and I was able to express myself much more. One of the joys of getting older is that you become far less afraid to say things, but I found myself being able to do that at a younger age.'

Perhaps part of being positive is to acknowledge the trigger that others can give to your own positive thinking. In this situation Helene, despite her apparent introverted nature, took the chance to experience something different in her life and was open-minded enough to allow an undiscovered part of her personality to come to the surface with the help of others.

Helene worked as a speech therapist, and then ran an art shop for 11 years, as well marrying and having two children. Her positive outlook had given her a fulfilling and very comfortable life so far, but she felt that her life could slowly slip away if she didn't make some positive decisions about how she would live the rest of it.

Taking opportunities

Helene's story began to resonate even more with me because as she got closer to the third 'post-work' age, she began to see that, health allowing, she had possibly 25 years of her life left and she wanted to make the most of them. She chose not to shy away from making some critical personal decisions (the second seminal moment). Helene knew that she had a deep need to generate something more meaningful and exploratory for herself, and she chose not to ignore what her instinct was telling her. She began to see that she had an opportunity to enrich her life rather than just letting the clock wind down. So instead of retiring to the country and a placid existence, she decided to go in the opposite direction, to London! She took an office job in her late fifties, working for several charities, and learnt lots about incompetent, unfeeling management and how this behaviour can have such a negative effect on people. She developed new skills too – learning to type and to use a computer.

Even with such a positive outlook and having taken such positive action, it can still be easy to slip back into 'life happens to me' habits. Helene's life had started to become sterile again until she listened to something a close friend told her. She was on a visit to Canada to see this old friend who had been a mentor to her and, just as she left, her friend (83 years old) told her she thought she might be getting a bit stale and perhaps it would be a good idea to open her mind a bit when she returned to London.

When she got back she heard a singer being interviewed on the radio. The singer said that most people can sing but don't because they think they can't or because they haven't tried. The next day she saw an ad in a shop window for a singer giving singing lessons. She connected the comments on the radio with the advertisement and, at 67 years old, she started singing lessons. She had a vague idea that she might join a choir, but went in with her eyes wide open. After three or four lessons it became apparent that not only could she sing, but that she could sing very well. Her teacher advised her to approach the London Philharmonic choir. So she did! When you audition, you are allowed one rehearsal and then you have the audition proper. Helene, believing rightly she had nothing to lose and everything to gain, chose to give her best and was offered a place in the choir.

Since that day Helene hasn't looked back. Now in her early seventies, she has travelled widely as part of the choir, going to places she never imagined she would see. Says Helene: 'It's been marvellous. I've been all over Europe and I've been to Asia too. I've always loved music and I never imagined at this stage of my life that it would be such a central part of it. I'm now thinking about the next thing I can do when I get to 80!' All with a little prompting from a friend and a willingness to try something new.

In many ways Helene had lived a comfortable life, but it was that very comfort that was perhaps stopping her from looking for more. When she did, she found another world there for her – from the small step of taking singing lessons. And who knows, there may be other worlds waiting to be explored.

Helene's experiences from the early and later parts of her life give us some valuable lessons whatever age we are:

■ If you assume you are a particular type of person, you are likely to behave in that way. If you tell yourself you are shy or that you aren't creative, for example, you are likely to follow your self-perception. Is your appraisal of 'you' accurate? Helene thought she was introverted and shy and then realized she wasn't!

■ When opportunities come along, think about them. Helene had two opportunities that may at the time have seemed quite small (and, of course, there were many more) and they both changed her life. What opportunities are you ignoring?

■ Sometimes we make the opportunity through our own positive, proactive decisions. Helene took the decision to have singing lessons. Where could you be more proactive?

■ Don't be afraid to take tough decisions. The short-term pain is wiped out by the long-term gain. Close to retirement, Helene didn't shy away from taking some critical personal decisions that changed the course of her life.

■ Good friends can sometimes see things in us that we don't. Don't dismiss their advice – even if it doesn't make for easy listening. Helene learnt from her good friend not to be afraid of trying new things, and to value the good things in life. Her friend is eyesight-blind but most definitely not insight-blind. What are your friends saying to you?

■ Gavin – Moving mountains

Gavin left university in 1987. The very next day he hitchhiked his way to Greece and from there worked on a tanker for six months and ended up in China. Nearly 20 years on, the adventure has never really ended. Gavin has scaled Everest, walked the Sahara Desert north to south alone, spent time in an Algerian jail accused of being a spy, and set up rehabilitation camps for street children in Nairobi. In a seminal achievement, Gavin scaled the seven highest peaks on the seven continents of the world in one year. He also finds time to run a company from Belfast called Adventure Alternative, which offers holidays in places that wouldn't be most people's number one destination of choice! A percentage of the profits from that company supports his charity for street kids in Nairobi.

There is one particular incident in Gavin's life that can give positive thinkers direction when circumstances challenge even the most positive of us – as Gavin himself says, 'where your situation can lead to a metaphorical crushing of the spirit'. In 2002 he and his climbing partner Will were 90 metres (300 feet) from the summit of Everest, climbing the north face, when Will dislocated his kneecap and was unable to walk. The chances of survival were virtually nil. Added to this, they were climbing without supplementary oxygen or support, which means that the body – and the mind – can be working at as little as 20 per cent efficiency. Over many days Gavin and Will managed to get themselves down to base camp. and in hindsight Gavin is able to pinpoint several factors that pulled them through their predicament.

1 Think with robot-like single-mindedness

In Gavin's circumstances the focus was first on staying alive and then on getting down the mountain. Finding yourself in a desperate situation means clearing the head of any psychological baggage and channelling your energy into one purpose. There are of course dangers here – maintaining perspective, for example – but in crises this single-minded thinking can work for us.

This single-mindedness applied to both Gavin and Will. Gavin is keen to stress that even though Will couldn't walk, it wasn't a question of Gavin 'saving' Will. If Will had placed the psychological burden on Gavin because of his physical condition, there is no way that either of them would have survived. They needed each other, and they needed each other to believe that they would make it.

2 Use intuition *and* rational thinking

In an unprecedented situation we need to draw on every last drop of our rational, reasoning, logical self to help us pull through. But sometimes thinking 'hard' fails to provide an answer, and we need our intuition to feel our way ahead. So it was that at the outset Gavin and Will had to make the emotional decision that they could get down together – even though the chances of success were against them. Then, once this decision had been made, they found themselves suppressing the emotional side of the brain. There was little room for sentiment – even when they saw several dead bodies on the way down.

Later in the book we see the value of positive thinkers acting as creative experimenters. However, there are times when this is important and times where things need to be done in a 'text-book' manner. In real crises, being conscious of the possible effects of each action can be critical. If you have the benefit of time (and we often have more time than we think), being realistic and mapping out the consequences of actions can reap dividends. Thinking positively can mean thinking realistically.

3 Exercise your 'will' power!

As fit as Gavin and Will were, they learnt very quickly that it wasn't their physical attributes that were the key to survival but rather how their thoughts could be translated into action. This reflects the experience of psychologist Viktor Frankl in Auschwitz: he noted that it was mental rather than physical strength that got inmates through hard labour in the concentration camp. Gavin and Will told themselves that they were going to get through this –

aware that the odds were stacked against them, they wanted to prove the statistics wrong. They talked themselves into a 'can do' frame of mind, with Will continually telling himself and Gavin, 'We can do this'.

> *The teamwork was so seamless and so tight that it's hard to*
> *separate the two of us out.*
>
> Gavin on his experience of climbing the north face of Everest with climbing partner Will

4 Ride with frustration

Success in these situations can frequently come from hard-headed realism. You need to understand that there will be setbacks, disappointments and frustrations: two steps forward, one step back. Preparing for setbacks and – this is crucial – believing you can overcome them, is what can often separate success from failure. The danger occurs when frustration or setback leads to a decline of will. It's often said that success in brutally challenging environments comes just beyond the point where most give up. As champion cyclist Lance Armstrong said: 'Pain is temporary, quitting is for ever.' Quitting really would have been for ever for Gavin and Will – this is a brutal environment to be in, and there are many instances of people being left behind and of climbers ignoring the stranded as they go past them.

Gavin told me that when they got back to base they both completely broke down – the suppressed emotional side of themselves burst out when they no longer needed the cool, rational thinking side. Proof, if need be, that we can hide our true feelings only for so long. In other environments it does no good to suppress this side – our true feelings leak out anyway.

The further adventures of Gavin

Fortunately, Gavin's vocation does not always consist of dealing with crises. His positive mental attitude as an adventurer challenges us all to think in more adventurous ways – even if our adventure isn't a physical one.

We could say why bother, why put yourself through this? The answer is that we all have our version of what adventure might mean. We can't apply to others our version of what it means to have a fulfilling life. If proof were needed to back up the 'uniqueness of you' mentioned in the Introduction, it is that if we all undertook the psychological journey that is the world of the positive thinker, all of our journeys would be different. The question for each of us is: do we want to make the journey?

We can read about Gavin and the places he has been to and delight in his adventures, thinking that it has little to do with us because maybe we don't have the capacity to do what he does. Or so we think. Gavin has created an adventure in his life that suits him. He has the capacity, as we all do, to be curious. What Gavin has done is to translate his own curiosity into a lifestyle for himself where he is almost continually challenged. The physical aspect of what he does is how his curious side manifests itself. As Gavin says, all his journeys in life begin 'between the ears' and he himself believes that whatever metaphorical journey you take in life, your capacity to get the most from it depends on the attitude you have to both your life and the lives of others when you begin it.

Gavin says this about his adventures:

> *They started off as dreams, idle thoughts on the back of a matchbox that developed through long days and nights to become a plan. And just imagine the joy, the satisfaction and the sense of living when those bold dreams became reality, rolled into new experiences and eventually turned to memories. For me, it gives life meaning. And not just for myself...*

What's intriguing about Gavin is that he isn't always obsessed with scaling the highest mountain or diving deeper than anyone in the ocean every time he sets out. As he says himself, 'Sometimes I just want to have an adventure.' The goals aren't always specific. Sometimes he jumps in and sees where the adventure takes him. Sometimes he has a specific target in mind.

From listening to Gavin's experiences, there are a number of themes that resonate strongly for us as positive thinkers:

1 Have a balance between goals and observation on journeys. Sometimes Gavin wants to scale the highest peak, sometimes he just wants to see what a particular place is like – the metaphorical 'dipping the toe in the water'.
2 Whatever you do, your attitude to the 'doing' is often the difference between success and failure.
3 Whatever your vocation, maintain your curiosity and the opportunities will

open up for you. When you are interested, things become more interesting.

4 There is an unlimited supply of unseen places to take yourself in the imagination – if you are willing to undertake the psychological journey.

5 Experience teaches us how to prepare for the journey but can never predict exactly what will happen. The 'surprise' is what makes life more interesting, but the surprise may also be the thing that challenges most deeply our capacity to be positive. Think about Gavin and Will's experience on Everest.

6 Shared experiences resonate strongly in the memory. Gavin and Will won't be forgetting each other!

■ Learning from 'real life'

The stories of each of our positive thinkers could fill a book. Their circumstances are all different; some of the advice conflicts, but what they've given us are four perspectives on what it means to think positively. Much of what they have said and done is developed and talked through in later chapters, with opportunities to apply some of the lessons to your own life. In fact, you may find it a useful exercise to write down the things that have particularly resonated with you in this chapter. I've offered examples of different situations in which positive thinking can work – getting through a crisis, working towards a particular goal, living a positive life, working with others, seeing and grasping opportunity, and trying new things to enrich your life.

What struck me about each of the people we've met in this chapter is that none of them is content to live on past achievements: there are many chapters in their respective life stories waiting to be written. Perhaps more than anything else, it is this desire to write new chapters that separates the high-level achievers in the world from the low-level. So are they special people? Of course they are! Does that mean that you are not special? Of course it doesn't! Don't try to copy what our four champions have done. They've found an arena in which they can express themselves. Your challenge is to find yours. It might be right in front of you in the work you do, or you might need to change a part of your life. Either way, you have the capacity in you to take yourself to the places you want to get to.

At the time of writing, Sergio is continuing his work fighting injustice and planning a trip to Spain, Gavin is half-way up a mountain, Helene is off to Singapore, and Kath is thinking how she can compete in the 2010 Winter Olympics. It would be hard to imagine any of them stopping until they've breathed their last breath!

Even though our positive thinkers have vastly different lives, they all share some characteristics:

■ None of them has a 'life happens to me' mentality. They all seem to be proactive, outward-looking. They get on with living.

■ They all value human relationships and acknowledge the contributions that others make to their lives. When I interviewed each of them it was interesting to note how keen they were to stress the contribution of others. For Kath, her parents and friends provided her with strong emotional support – they had all told her she was exactly the right person to undertake such a hard physical test. For Sergio it has been his wife of over 30 years, Eugenia, whom he describes as 'a Mediterranean hurricane' – she's half Catalan and half Italian. For Helene it was her friend in Canada who put her back on the rails when she was drifting. For Gavin it was an acknowledgement of the importance of the team in expeditions – even though he is the leader – and the support and encouragement of Will in the effort to save themselves near the top of Everest.

■ They all have a degree of single-mindedness that helps them in what they do, but they are adaptable when they need to be.

■ They are curious. They all look for opportunities to develop and grow. For Sergio it was education. For Kath it was the chance to test her level of mental and physical capability. For Helene it was learning to sing. For Gavin it is always the next adventure.

The most horrifying thing in the world is to be without adventure.

George Foreman, boxer and entrepreneur

Chapter 2
Travelling to other worlds

❏ Outside in

❏ Psychological travel

❏ A ticket for today's travel

❏ Our fellow travellers

❏ Child's fare

❏ A short journey – 'interiority'

❏ Free travel – a 'GIFT'

■ Outside in

Helen Sharman was the first British woman in space. Floating high above the Earth with only the companionship of two Soviet cosmonauts, she was able to place herself on the outside looking in – able to see our planet from a spot beyond it. When she looked back at it, the first thing she noticed was its beauty. The pristine clarity of 'the blue planet' has resonated with her long after her return and she says she will never forget it. For the first and probably only time in her life she was able to appreciate our home in its full majesty.

We don't have to go into space to get an alternative view of the world. Being able to stand on the outside and 'look in' is important if we want to see the opportunities that life lays open for us. It means stepping out of our existing life and seeing how each of us resonates with the bigger thing of which we are a part – a world of people, places and things.

This is a very early step in developing a more positive outlook: being able to step back and use the full breadth of our imagination to leapfrog the daily gripes and problems that can, if we are not careful, take us over.

Adventurers like Gavin in the previous chapter can take themselves to places physically and psychologically that are frequented by few of us, and, when there, begin to see a beautiful picture that most of us, living our life in the smaller details, are unaware of. We live in a micro-world and have, knowingly or not, shut off the possibilities of a macro one.

What's fascinating about adventurers is that before they begin a new journey they can only imagine what their destination feels and looks like. What drives them is that their fertile imagination takes over early and they see the possibilities of physical travel and personal discovery. Our journey in this chapter is not about physical adventure, but more about applying the mentality of the physical adventurer to our capacity as positive thinkers to 'psychologically travel' – that is, to open up the possibilities of the future through our curiosity and our imagination.

It has been said that the fourth primal human driver, along with food, sex and shelter, is curiosity. It is, however, the one that we frequently choose to deny ourselves. If we accept things as they seem to be, we live our life according to what we think is real, and these opinions could have been formed at a very young age. If we are curious about why things are the way we think they are, we often discover that they aren't. Our personal world of possibilities can be so much more enriching if we are curious about it. It's tempting but unrewarding to choose a limiting world-view because it's 'easy'.

When Ellen MacArthur completed her single-handed sail around the world in 2005 in record time there were many who belittled her achievement, saying she had relied on technology rather than sailing skills. Others just wondered, 'Why bother?' A reader of the *Independent* sent a letter to the paper reminding people of this quote by mountaineer George Leigh Mallory:

> *If you cannot understand that there is something [in us] which responds to the challenge of this mountain and goes out to meet it, that the struggle is the struggle of life itself upward, then you won't see why we go. What we get from this adventure is just sheer joy. And joy is, after all, the end of life. We do not live to eat and make money. We eat and make money to be able to enjoy life. That is what life means and what life is meant for.*

Many of us have a spirit of adventure. The challenge for positive thinkers is to express our curiosity outwardly rather than keeping it suppressed within us.

■ Psychological travel

> *This sort of enforced looking is, I realize, comparatively rare in our lives: on the whole we seek out the things we are already interested in. Our habits of inspection and our view of the world are re-confirmed each time we concentrate our vision or avert our eye.*
> Julian Barnes, *Letters from London*

Our own journey in life need not be a physical one: the destination might be a career move, learning new skills or adjusting to parenthood but, like the adventurer, we can begin to see the possibilities of mentally taking ourselves to unseen places if we want. The challenge is to construct positive possibilities in our mind, and for this we need some opportunity-spotting tools to help us.

Psychological travel kicks in when we use our imagination to take ourselves into situations we may want to experience in the future – when we take ourselves mentally to new places that might create new opportunities. It is only the self-imposed limit on our imagination that prevents us from seeing infinite possibilities. The physical traveller seeks new adventure and so does the psychological traveller. Our possibilities might exist in any part of life but they need to be found. If we shut off our imagination we won't see them.

Adults often tell children: 'The world is your oyster'. Some say it because they are encouraging young people to see the world that way and because they still apply that thinking to their own life. Others, however, say it because they believe they have had their life, that the opportunities for them have gone and that the opportunity baton is being handed down to others. Why and when did this self-imposed barrier get built?

The biggest barrier we face is that we believe that our current circumstances make exploring pointless. Think of those times when we say: 'I don't have the time', 'I've got kids', 'My job is too demanding', 'I'm in debt' and so on. In this situation we can try to flip our thinking on its head. Instead of getting into a 'what I can't do' mentality and producing a huge list of blocks, try 'what I can do' thinking. Think of J.K. Rowling, who, despite (that word 'despite' is another self-imposed barrier!) single motherhood, decided to write a book. She told herself she *could* write a book.

Make your own list of possibilities. Note down 100 things you could do, and don't be judgemental at this stage. Just get your ideas down on paper.

Having produced a list of possibilities, ask 'Why not?' Sometimes there will be restrictions, but often those restrictions will be self-imposed.

▪ A ticket for today's travel

> *Animals do not exist by being, they exist by happening... An animal is like a whirlpool; it derives its relative stability, and even its form, from its motion, and it is only kept moving through its interactions with the wider system of which it is a part.*
> Psychologist Guy Claxton, *Noises from the Darkroom*

It's the interaction with our world and the people in it that creates meaning and keep us moving forward. The wider system to which Guy Claxton refers comprises people, nature and things, together with many realities that our knowledge of science has not stretched to yet. In the following section we look at one aspect of the 'wider system' – the people who comprise it.

As curious psychological travellers, we cannot do without people. At our best we are inspiring, exciting, diverse, giving and a remarkable source of knowledge. At our worst – well, we all know the bad bits! Being a psychological traveller means using our imagination like an internet search engine. When we search on the internet we enter the name of the thing we're searching for, or the idea we've got that we want to find out more about, or the name of the person we're interested in. We get presented with hundreds or maybe even thousands of possibilities for further searching. It's a bit like that with our imagination too. When we decide to access a particular site from our searching we increase our knowledge about the thing we were searching for and it may be that that particular site has links to other sites. In the same way our brain can make all sorts of links and connections if we provide the initial thinking to kick-start it. The possibilities really do become endless.

We can seek to understand the worlds of those around us better too. We can be curious about people – about how they think, act, feel, intuit, believe. Exercising this curiosity helps us see the possibilities of an open world rather than the restrictions of a closed one because we are actively engaging with that world. Almost everything we do in life comes from interactions with people – personal relationships, working relationships, job interviews, leisure activities and so on. It is, however, easy to say 'find out more', and a bigger step to overcome the barriers that restrict our ability to search.

So what are these barriers? And how do we overcome them? These are questions we can try to answer in the rest of this chapter.

■ Our fellow travellers
A barrier presents itself when our unacknowledged prejudices are allowed to strangle ideas or sever the connection between people, ideas and the opportunities of the future. The barrier normally begins with the first of these – people. And it's our own prejudices that prevent us from looking at the unique perspective that each person gives to the world.

Keeping an open mind
When we first meet someone our mind works overtime to categorize and stereotype that person. These categories are usually based around our own

prejudices. Think about the times when we check into a hotel or walk into a restaurant and we are immediately making judgements about the receptionist or the waiter based on how they look. They are doing the same with us! Initially our descriptions will be based around vague words – 'interesting', 'boring', 'dull' and 'creative', for example. We may even have formed these opinions before we met the person – someone will have told us about them before the first meeting.

For example, if we know 'something' about somebody, our first conversation with them is immediately prejudiced because we find ourselves reacting to the 'something' rather than the person – particularly if we don't know that person well. We can practise this ourselves. Pick a sport. If we know someone who likes that sport, do we immediately build up a mental picture of the person based on that snippet of information? Have a look at the list of sports below and at some of the views that might be expressed about the people who like them:

Sport	People who like this sport...
Beach volleyball	... are vacuous, lack depth
Cricket	... are boring
Basketball	... like instant gratification
Shooting	... like killing things
Lacrosse	... are English public-school types

And people who like sport full stop? Male!

Of course, some of these comments may reflect my prejudices – hard as I try to contain them, they leak out. But if I make these assumptions about people professing likes in these areas, I am immediately prejudicing any conversation I have with any of them because I am building up a mental picture of that person – hanging on to fragments of information in which to make the picture more real. I meet someone who enjoys beach volleyball and I immediately think 'lacks depth' and I look for signals that confirm that initial impression rather than looking for contrary evidence.

An extra dimension of this is that we will be initially attracted to the person who is 'like me' because there is a shared interest. That interest may last, but needs to be balanced by not dismissing those who are apparently 'not like me' because we don't think they offer anything for us. In fact, the opposite may be the case. These searching skills are essential because if we don't look, we are shutting off the key pathway to an improved relationship with the world.

Our prejudices have been formed by a raft of early influences: culture, schooling, parents and friends. We see these prejudices as 'normal' because it's what we know, it's common sense. But, as Albert Einstein once said, common sense is the set of prejudices we acquire before the age of 18. We can spend our life according to those prejudices – or challenging them:

■ See more than you have already 'seen'

Don't reaffirm your own stereotype of a person by listening only to the things that confirm it. Once we've begun to paint a picture of a particular person, there's no stopping us! We'll be looking out for as many signals as we possibly can that confirm this initial view and blanking out those that don't 'fit'. If we go abroad on holiday or for work, we look out for the signals that confirm the stereotypical images we have of other nationalities.

■ Seek contrary 'evidence'

OK, so we're talking to someone who likes cricket. Some of us, American readers particularly, may find cricket 'boring' (or is that another gross author stereotype?) because a game can last five days. But, by probing a little more, we find that the person also likes to take part in stock-car racing or mountain climbing. Probe a little more and we find that the person is an artist and likes to paint while there is something going on around them that doesn't take up too much of their attention – hence their enjoyment of watching cricket. By asking questions to seek contrary evidence we build up a much more realistic, balanced picture.

■ Are they telling you what they think you want to hear?

In male-dominated companies it is often said that the key to success for a woman is to take on the characteristics of the male worker so as not to draw too much attention to the fact that she is 'different'. Women perceive, perhaps rightly, that this 'difference' is too much of a challenge to the male environment. By saying the things that they imagine a more senior male wants to hear they hope to make progress. By failing to explore the side of women that makes them different from men, this company is failing to utilize the talents of 50 per cent of the population – all too true in many organizations.

▦ Warts and all!

It's said that as positive thinkers we should surround ourselves with like-minded people because having negativity around us can damage our own positive thinking mindset. We pick up the human equivalent of 'negative ions'. But how realistic is that? Are we wanting to live our life in a goldfish bowl or to be a world citizen, warts and all? In reality we are not likely to be able to 'choose' everyone we associate with for any period of time, and we could miss out on valuable experiences if we opt to do so.

Most of us can't choose whom we work with, who is sitting at the next restaurant table or who our team-mates are in the basketball team. What we can choose is the attitude we have to those around us. Positive thinkers seek to bring those around them 'up' rather than bring themselves 'down'. Positive thinking is not a selfish mental pursuit.

Why not try this? The next time you meet someone whom you know you will be spending time with (a new work colleague perhaps), why not test out and improve your own skills as a people explorer? The first time you meet them write a list of their perceived likes and dislikes (sport, cars, etc.) and a few words on their personality. Spend the next week finding contrary evidence and make a note of all the things you find out about them. How close was your first impression? Your initial list is likely to be a long way from reality, but your subsequent behaviour with that person may well be based on your first impression.

> *Sometimes we think we are thinking, when we are merely rearranging our prejudices.*
> Psychologist William James

▦ Child's fare

What can we learn from children? Opposite are two observations that may help us to see what the child's view of the world can give to us as adults: ·

1 *Play School*

In the 1970s there was a UK children's television programme where the presenter asked the children watching which window they wanted to look through – the round, square or arched window. Each window had an 'on location' report from a zoo or a toy factory or an underwater expedition behind it – something that would capture the imagination of the children watching. The presenter would look at the camera and ask the hypothetical child watching at home, 'Which window?' and then answer the question themselves: 'Today it is the arched window,' for example. Of course, most children watching were playing the game, trying to guess correctly, while at the same time asking, 'Why can't I look through all three?' Children have great search engines, furnished by an almost never-ending curiosity.

2 I really *want* to play

About 20 years ago a very funny writer about creative thinking, Roger von Oech, wrote a terrific book, *A Whack on the Side of the Head*. In it he gave an example of the differences in mindset between adults and children. He tells the story of a teacher with a group of adult students. The teacher puts a black splodge on the board and asks the group what it is, to which they reply, 'A black splodge.' The teacher is surprised, telling them that if she showed the image to a group of children, they'd come up with all sorts of answers – a squashed fly, a hole, part of a Dalmatian dog and so on.

Twenty years on, do we think that adults would still reply in the same way? We've become more aware of our creative possibilities, and in tests I've conducted adults come up with a whole host of answers. But there is still one difference between the adults and the children. The children are still excited by the idea of coming up with solutions – even at such a young age it can turn into a competitive challenge. The adults, however (with exceptions), 'play the game' but almost because it's expected of them, not because they think they have can a bit of fun for two minutes. It's as if they say, 'This is a creative thinking exercise, so this is the way I am expected to behave for the next two minutes.' Thinking creatively has become as much of a chore for some as thinking itself.

Of course, as positive thinkers we are often being challenged to adopt the mind of a child, and there are good reasons at times not to – particularly when deadlines need to be adhered to or when we become curious for the sake of it. But there are two things we can learn from our children:

▦ Only you have the set of keys to your imagination

The parameters in which we utilize our personal 'search engine' for possibility or opportunity are almost limitless. Indeed, the only limits are either self-imposed or culturally imposed. No one else has a set of keys to your imagination, and within that imagination you are completely free to explore opportunities. To use our example of the children's programme, you don't need to choose a window at the search stage – the real skill is in recognizing that you have a choice of windows.

▦ Give your heart as well as your head

Like the adult today looking at the black splodge, we are much better at playing the creativity game than we used to be. But the willingness to engage with a problem or situation is the variable here. Putting the heart as well as the head into it pushes us that much further – to the solution at the limit of our thinking rather than to a solution shared with others. Our heart gives us a deeper level of emotional engagement. Sometimes, of course, the easy solution will be just fine. At other times something deeper will be needed.

▦ A short journey – 'interiority'

We've looked in this chapter at how, as positive thinkers, we can travel psychologically – looking for possibilities in our world. We can be curious, asking all the right questions, but are we listening to the answers?

In his great novel *Microserfs*, based in 1990s' Silicon Valley corporate culture, Douglas Coupland invented a wonderful new word – 'interiority':

> *Learnt a new word today: 'Interiority' – it means being inside somebody's head.*

Coupland was referring to the curiosity required to get into the interior of other people's minds – interior curiosity.

Our challenge is to seek the 'interiority complex'. If we believe that there are 6 billion worlds out there – that everyone is truly different – then the challenge, as a listener, is to be curious enough to investigate the complex interior that is another person's world. To develop your 'interiority complex' skills.

The benefits of being a great listener are huge whether you are listening or being listened to. As true psychological travellers, we seek knowledge and understanding of the world. Listening – and learning – from others is an integral part of that process. You cannot truly understand your opinions, prejudices and world view unless you appreciate the worlds of others. It's important to be able to filter your own thinking through the minds and thoughts of others. Here are some other benefits:

■ Opportunities in life often come from the ideas and inspiration of others. Lack of listening shuts off an avenue of opportunity.
■ As positive thinkers, we have a lifelong commitment to learning – both about the world we inhabit and the inhabitants of that world.
■ We don't live in a world where we say things and people go off and do them. We need to be assertive (not aggressive), to influence, to negotiate. Listening underpins our ability to be effective in each of these core skills.

Effective listening is key for our work too. Think about how great listening helps in these environments:

■ Sales people who need to get into the 'heads' of their clients.
■ Managers who mistakenly think that one approach to managing fits all.
■ Individuals who work with people from diverse cultural backgrounds.
■ Advertising/marketing staff who need to know their 'market'.
■ People who serve 'customers'.
■ People who work abroad.

What stops us being able to truly listen, to project ourselves into other psychological worlds, is hampered by what's going on in our mind as we ostensibly 'listen'.

Losing 'me'
Remember that time you were the only person in the house and you were cooking or doing the housework? You had some of your favourite music on,

quite loud, and you were beginning to lose yourself in it – to the point where you were becoming the person on the CD/tape/record. And suddenly you were that person. The rolling pin became the microphone...the broom became the guitar. You lost yourself and forgot 'you'. You were in the head of the singer or musician you were listening to.

It's interesting how many people I know who do this. They tell me they often put the music back on right away when it's finished and lose themselves again!

Losing 'you' is a crucial part of effective listening. When we listen there is a tendency to continue to have an internalized conversation with yourself as you prepare to reply – that's the point where you stop listening to the other person. As the author of *The Seven Habits of Highly Effective People*, Stephen Covey, puts it:

> *We typically seek first to be understood. Most people do not listen with the intent to understand – they listen with the intent to reply. They're either speaking or preparing to speak. They're filtering everything through their own paradigms, reading their autobiography into other people's lives.*

Conversation can often become a competitive exercise – 'I did this...' may be counteracted with a 'Well, I did this...' It's a tricky situation: we want to tell the other person all about 'me' because our ego demands it, but we have to suppress this tendency if we truly want to understand where the other person is coming from. When we feel we have this understanding, we are in a better position to relate what we are saying to the world of the other person. And, if we need to, we are also able to present our opinion in a language and framework they can understand because we now understand their world.

We can think of effective listening as a bit like peeling onions. Think of the person you are interacting with as an onion. The 'onion' has layer upon layer offering up complexity upon complexity, and your challenge is to peel back the layers so that you can truly understand that person.

Two can play that game

This is an exercise that needs a friend or colleague. Take a piece of paper and cut a letterbox-size piece out of the middle of it. Then hold a conversation with the friend or colleague while looking through the 'hole' – you should try to manoeuvre it in such a way that you cannot see anything else apart from their face. After a few giggles you'll be amazed how attentive to your partner you become. At first you notice everything about their physiognomy. Funny pimples, discoloration, make-up, all the colours in the eye and so on.

Keep going with the conversation. Once the novelty of physiognomy has worn off, you find yourself locking into what the other person is saying. Every other distraction is shut off. At that moment they are the most important person in the world. And you are to them. Try to keep it like that.

What you are doing is shutting out two of the key barriers to effective listening. The first is the shutting out of all peripheral distractions. The view out of the window behind your colleague may be interesting but you can't see it, so you are concentrating on them…just them.

The second is eye contact. One of the biggest giveaways that someone is not listening is that they fail to maintain eye contact. But a word of warning. Don't turn this into a stare-out – just enough eye contact that the other person knows they are the centre of your attention.

Remember these key points – they'll help us all become better listeners:

- **Project yourself** into the other person's mind – what are they really thinking?
- **Seek to understand** – you can understand your own thinking better if you understand the thinking of others.
- **Change your perceptual filter** – different perceptions give the positive thinker a wider parameter of understanding.
- **Escape from the prison** of your own self-perception.
- **Avoid verbal sparring** – conversation is not competition.
- **Use silence** as thinking time. In many Asian countries people are quite happy with silence (for thinking time) in conversation. In Western societies people think they always have to fill the gap.
- Disagree with yourself by seeking **contrary evidence** from others.
- Listeners **ask questions** that get more than 'yes' or 'no' answers.
- Imagine you are individually **removing the layers** of an onion. Have you got to the last layer?
- **Confirm back** to the person what you think you have heard.

And finally, consider this. Are we not inclined to remember the people who listened to us when we needed them to? Great friend, great manager or parent? The internal force that is positive thinking manifests itself in our attitude to the world and the people in it. Give people time and they'll give you time. In human relationships you reap what you sow.

■ Free travel – a 'GIFT'

Me, We

Muhammad Ali

Positive thinking uses the language of 'me' and the language of 'we' too. 'I' is most people's favourite word in the English language! Remember the great spoof character Ali G – 'I is not happy' with the emphasis on the 'I'. 'Me' and 'we' mean not just about 'me' but also how one sees the world and the people in it – how we relate to the people in 'our' world; seeing 'me' as part of something bigger. The more we give to that world the more we get in return. As positive thinkers we look to grow the adventurous spirit in us. And that spirit of adventure extends to our relationships with other people.

We come to one of the core principles of the positive thinker – seeing others as a GIFT to us rather than a hindrance to our enjoyment of the world. When it comes down to it, without other people there is no world. The GIFT has a double meaning because it also serves as handy mnemonic:

G   Get
I   It
F   From
T   Them

We can see the things people say and do as a GIFT to us.

Seeking the GIFT (through great listening, suspension of prejudice or stereotypical imaging) provides us with the purity test for our own:

■ opinions
■ prejudices
■ perspectives
■ world-view.

But the GIFT also provides us with:

- opportunities – this doesn't mean 'using' other people
- stronger personal relationships
- extra sets of antennae that help us to see more options and choices.

The GIFT allows us to filter our own thinking through the lives and thinking of others and challenges us to see the world in other ways. We can't change who's in the picture of our life, at least not in the short term, but we can change the way we actually look at that picture.

Ultimately, it may be true to say that our life is defined as much by relationships and the meaning we attach to those relationships. In her book *I Don't Know How She Does It* author Alison Pearson says:

> *In death we are not defined by what we did or who we are but by what we meant to others. How well we loved and were loved in return.*

We can dispute this sentiment, but find an aspiration and indeed a beauty in it. Ultimately, it probably depends on who we want to be remembered by, but we only have to think about the people from our past who have had an influence on us and we immediately come to those who gave us love and the expressions of that – time, trust, caring and commitment.

Early in our adult lives, as we are trying to find our place in the world, many of us will have had a mentor, a relative or maybe a caring manager, who gave us their time and from whom we learnt more about the world and how we might succeed in it. They listened and helped us and we both grew from the relationship. Being chosen as a mentor by someone (and we can only be 'chosen') is one of the greatest gifts that a person can bestow on you.

We've taken many journeys in this chapter. We've taken the short journey into the life and world of our fellow travellers. We've taken longer trips to the world of endless possibility and opportunity. These 'travelling skills', where we seek a life of mental and/or physical adventure, take time to develop. It is unlikely that we will jump from the stopping service to the fast train at the flick of a switch. Try taking a small step first – perhaps a short journey to the world of fellow trvellers – and see where the first journey takes you.

Light my fire, or so the song says – but the true firelighters live inside my head.

Chapter 3
Feeding the fire

❏ Opportunity knocks

❏ Learning to learn

❏ Learning to be optimistic

❏ Building confidence

Each of us has our own internal fire. This fire energizes us. Different people have different-size flames – the flames we were born with. We can't worry about what we were born or not born with because we can't do anything about it. What we can do is make use of some practical ideas that help us to turn our flame into a healthy fire that really drives us on. It's a bit like a reptile in an open space. No warmth or little sun, and its blood stays cold and it can't move about. The sun comes out and it's on the move.

The idea that we are all motivated is disputed by some. But think about all the things we do that require motivation – even just getting out of bed, cooking a meal or walking to the shops. Add a little bit extra (get the personal flame burning brighter) and look at what can be added:

Action	Extra heat
Getting out of bed	Rising early
Cooking an omelette	Adding potatoes and onions, and making a Spanish omelette
Walking to the shops	Cycling to the shops
Going to watch a game	Playing the game
Buying a Christmas present	Buying a gift when we don't have to
Sitting an exam	Passing an exam

Why not add some of your own here? Actions you undertake that, with a little bit more, become something bigger for you. What could that 'bigger' be?

In this chapter we look at four mindsets that can help us make the most of the capacity for being positive that exists in all of us. These mindsets provide us with the edge that allows us to make best use of the part of us that desires to be positive. These are:

- Searching out and taking opportunity.
- Commitment to personal learning and development.
- Being optimistic.
- Building confidence.

In the next chapter we dig a little deeper – into parts of us that may take many years to fully understand. By consciously starting to think about these we get to the point where we can use this deeper understanding for personal benefit more quickly:

- self-knowledge/knowing me
- using intuition
- whole...heart...head...ness.

Opportunity knocks

In the last chapter we looked at the possibilities of psychological travel – how we use our imagination to think up future possibilities for ourselves. Opening up our imagination is crucial for the creating of opportunities too, because we are able to embrace the potential in the world rather than shy away from it. It helps us as positive thinkers to make the effort to seek out opportunity as well as enjoying the randomness of opportunities presenting themselves. In the random world it's how receptive we are to opportunity that's key – as psychological travellers, we create the conditions for ourselves where the imagination visualizes opportunity from the tiniest spark, but the mind is wide and receptive enough to see what's really there. I don't mean to be frivolous when I say that opportunities come at us like space rocks passing the Starship *Enterprise*. We cannot hope to catch all the rocks (or even see all of them) because there are so many. It is a sad reality that many people barely take the opportunity to look out of the window.

It's the difference between going through life with your eyes wide open and choosing to hide in a cave when the sun comes out. In affluent societies we can become victim to the eighth deadly sin: apathy. Or to expand it further: the apathy of opportunity. Because in childhood, adolescence and beyond it has been comparatively easy for many of us, we can take for granted the things that people in other, less privileged, cultures would grasp. Having spent time in environments such as Kosovo and Georgia with desperately high levels of unemployment (up to 85 per cent), I have observed and delighted in the energy committed by those who have even the smallest window of opportunity to the few chances they get. In post-industrial cultures we need to guard against taking these opportunities for granted. Sometimes we manage to convince ourselves that these opportunities are not even there or are the preserve of the few.

Saeed's story

I feel a bit uncomfortable saying this really because I'm grateful for the opportunities I've had in my new home and I don't want to seem critical because I'm really not. I came from Pakistan to the UK in the late 1980s and the motivation for me and many of my friends to do this was the opportunities we can have here. When you come from my country, you tend to recognize an opportunity when you see it because we have far fewer chances than people in Western countries. For many of my fellow countrymen the priorities are much more basic because opportunities are limited. A few years ago I had a chance to go to the UK. I have to admit it was through luck rather than my own efforts, but I took the chance right away. I think I have an adventurous spirit, and although I loved my home, and still do, I wanted something else. I have been in my new home for a few years now and I've been someone from the outside looking in.

I do get a bit angry when I see so many people in the West taking for granted the amazing opportunities they have. Let me give an example. Just think: here we can educate ourselves in almost any subject, at any age, for very little money. Sometimes for free, sometimes government or employers pay, but for most people learning new things can come very cheaply at almost any age. Where I come from we have education, but it can be a real struggle. And yet here we see so many people abusing it or ignoring it. I remember in the early 1990s when computers started to be used more and more at work that some of my work colleagues were struggling to use them because they didn't know how to. Some of them saw them as a threat. And yet night schools were offering courses in computing skills very cheaply, and in fact our employer was offering basic computing skills for almost everyone. It was easier to complain about computers than see the opportunity that the new technology presented.

It's not for me to preach to the country that's given me a chance to make my way because I'm grateful for the chances I've had. But I think that sometimes when there is so much, we almost become blind to it. Because of this I find myself doing certain things. I am incredibly positive about each day. When I wake up I try and make a conscious decision to do something or to achieve something in that day. And now I have children I try to get them to appreciate what they have. I get frustrated when all they want to do is watch TV! I just want to tell them to get out there and take the opportunities.

In the Personal Resources section (see page 181, Exercise 1) you'll find 21 statements relating to opportunity-spotting. You have the option to do this short exercise now. It will take five to ten minutes and its value comes in helping us to think more about our own potential for creating, spotting and acting on opportunities.

Readers who do the exercise will then be familiar with the statements below, but don't worry if you haven't done the exercise because explanations are provided. All of them can help us as opportunity-spotters to think positively about seeing and taking opportunities. Sometimes we can make a strong case for opposite arguments in these statements. Perhaps the key here, if we want both to spot and seize opportunities, is to keep the mind flexible so that we can weigh up the options. The more experiences we create for ourselves, the more we are likely to be able to use intuition to guide us.

As you read the statements below, try to think of examples of each that apply to your own life.

1 Some opportunities are there for me for only a very short time
Some opportunities exist for us for an extended period, perhaps even for our whole life. Others, particularly those based on chance encounters with other people, may exist for only a short time. Did you ever catch somebody's eye when you were on the down escalator and they were going up? And did you think, 'If only…'?

2 I know myself – sometimes opportunities need to be right for me
There is little point in joining the army if you find it difficult to take orders and dislike too much routine. Best fit is good, but don't underestimate your capacity to adapt. You may find out things about yourself you never knew!

3 Sometimes the answer is right in front of me
…but I'm looking so hard elsewhere I don't see it! Opportunity-spotters wear lenses for short and long sightedness.

4 I look for possibilities rather than waiting for them
We said earlier that the theatre of life is not the sofa. On the other hand, we need to slow down sometimes so that things can catch up with us.

5 My curiosity creates opportunities for me

A searching mentality takes us into previously unexposed (to us) parts of the world. Being curious for the sake of the experience is fine. Being curious because we want to lift the lid off the opportunity tin takes us a lot further than just an experience.

6 I have multiple options – there is always more than one potential opportunity

Most problems have a multitude of solutions even though we often convince ourselves that there is only one course of action. The solutions to problems often provide us with a wider arc of opportunity.

7 Sometimes I need to break out of conventional wisdom

If we all worked according to conventional wisdom we'd restrict the possibility for invention, innovation and creativity – all three of which sow the seeds for new opportunities.

8 I am a realist – opportunities present obstacles too

And here lies the challenge. How much do we really want to take up the opportunity? Enough that we want to overcome the obstacles, or not enough that we think the effort required would be worth it?

9 Changes bring me opportunities

It is often said that in the world of corporate mergers, takeovers and buyouts, the lucky ones are those who get made redundant. But really the survivors are those who see opportunity whether they get retained or made redundant – the ones who create their own luck whatever their circumstances.

10 I'm less likely to see opportunity when I'm not looking

The opportunity may think we don't like it, so it ignores us. It's the same with people.

11 Routine can lead to less opportunity-spotting

It's easy to slip in the comfort zone and become part of the system. Making a conscious decision to operate in that way is fine, but slipping into routine absent-mindedly makes it harder to for us to break out and seize opportunity.

12   With opportunities, sometimes if I let the lid off, I can't put it back on again – things have changed for ever
If you run after the person on the escalator, your life may never be the same again! Be prepared for the upheaval that opportunity-taking can bring.

13 I've had great ideas – they just didn't seem that way at the time
Hindsight isn't really a wonderful thing. Opportunity-takers use 'What if?/Why not' language to help them create possibilities rather than regrets.

14 Too much analysis – and I might talk myself out of it
Remember the golfer or the tennis player who spent so long analysing their game that they became paralysed by the fear of doing something incorrectly? Allowing for spontaneity helps to sharpen our instincts and keep us 'fresh'. Always allow for instinct and 'gut' feeling.

15 I avoid using 'if only' statements – what's gone has gone
Regretting the past is misdirected thinking. Learning from past mistakes directs our thinking into future focus.

16 Learning new things creates possibilities for me
In reality we continue to learn as our life progresses, and we often absorb that learning without thinking about it. Look back at your life over the last six months and make a list of the new things you've learnt (the list is likely to be enormous). What possibilities does this new knowledge present for you?

17 Opportunities can be created from my own imagination
Imagining future scenarios for ourselves takes us nearer to reaching them. Have another look at Chapter 2 for the possibilities of psychological travel.

18 I anticipate opportunities rather than reacting to them
Visualizing possibilities puts you closer to creating them. Sometimes we don't see what's coming and reacting positively is fine. At other times 'thinking ahead' can pay dividends.

19 I am as prepared as I can be to make the most of my opportunities
We'll never be completely prepared (see below). Remember that if we seek complete information on which to make opportunity-taking decisions, we may never have enough. At some point we all have to jump. Or not.

20 Opportunities may become problems if I don't act on them
If someone else seizes the opportunity, they may create a problem for us. Our world may have changed because of their opportunity-taking. Even if this doesn't happen, our failure to act early may create a big problem later.

21 I like the uncertainty that opportunity-taking can bring
Opportunity can bring uncertainty, ambiguity and contradiction. If we are prepared for that, we may feel more comfortable in unstable worlds and better able to take the opportunities we have.

Opportunity dismissed?
The language we use indicates the mindset we have when we take or spurn opportunities. Is your language opportunity-building or barrier-growing?

Positive language	Building barriers
Some opportunities are only there briefly and we have to be alert to them.	I didn't have the time.
I try to break out of conventional wisdom.	Things are fine as they are.
Sometimes the answers are right in front of me.	I never got a break.
I like searching around in new areas.	I know what I like.
I seek out opportunity.	If opportunity comes my way, then fine.
Sometimes when you start it's impossible to stop.	I don't like taking risks.
I can overcome those barriers.	There are barriers?
Sometimes you need to go for it.	I sometimes talk myself out of doing things.
What are the possibilities?	What might I lose?
Why not?	If only…

■ Learning to learn

Imagine the first time you did something – perhaps learning to swim or drive a car. How did it feel? Did you grasp it quickly or struggle to acquire this new skill? The issue is not whether you succeeded or failed, but whether what you felt caused your success or failure. Over the last 50 years psychologists and 'thinkers' have explored why it is that some people succeed and others seem to fail – or, more specifically, to what they attribute their success or failure. In what's become known as 'causality', we seek to attribute reasons for things happening – why, for example, is it that I am or am not mastering the art of learning to drive, or why is it that others are or aren't learning to drive? Why do some of us see ourselves as high-level achievers and behave accordingly, and some as low-level achievers (which means low in comparison to what we are capable of) and again carry this perception as a personal fault-line?

Let's take learning to drive as an example because it is a skill many of us have had to acquire. We start with the person who is struggling to acquire this new skill. Ultimately, learning to drive may depend on what they perceive as the reason for the struggle. This is not to say that the person with initial failure characteristics will fail. How many of us have that initial 'this is impossible' feeling when confronted with something new and apparently complex to deal with? A mini success plants the seeds of possibility in our mind and we are then up and running. In Kath's story in Chapter 1, she was able to beat an experienced skier in the British Cross-country Skiing Championships after only three weeks' practice (page 30). She was able to use that mini success to build her confidence and make her believe that she was heading in the right direction.

Every small positive step on the way to learning something new can cancel out the negative feelings we may have had before. Feeling helpless or hopeless is understandable but – and this is crucial – none of us is a failure. Failing does not make you a failure. Succeeding at something, anything, makes you a success. Once we've had success we can use it to feed into the next stage of our learning. Success breeds confidence. When learning something new it helps to recognize that learning is usually done in stages. Expecting to learn to drive right away is unrealistic.

Where this breaks down is when we believe that success, no matter how small, is due to things that have nothing to with our own capability – we say that our success is due to external factors, quite often 'luck'. Let's examine the sort of personal language that may help us to succeed or hold us back as we attempt to learn to drive.

High achievement	Possibility of under-achievement
This will take practice.	I want to know now.
I need to listen to my instructor and ask questions.	My instructor is no good.
Hey, I've learnt to change gear.	But that's the easy stuff.
I did it! (on passing your test)	The examiner caught me on a good day.

What am I saying?

When developing new skills, write down the words that are going through your head as you do so. What we say to ourselves about our capacity for improvement in this new skill area will be fundamental to our acquiring this new skill or not.

If you're struggling, is it because the conversation you're having with yourself is based around negative thoughts?

Learning to drive successfully is an example of something that nearly every person is keen to do (I hope even non-driving readers will appreciate the example used) and it provides very powerful lessons about the learning process that many will identify with. Many of us are prepared to fail our test three, four or five times before we pass because the desire to succeed over-comes the knockback of failure. Where else would we be prepared to absorb this level of lack of success and still come back for more? Learn from the fact that a very high percentage of you reading this passed in the end. Where else could you apply this 'drive for success' mindset in your life? And to those of you who never mastered driving, there will be many other things you have learnt to do successfully where you displayed the profile of the high achiever in abundance. Being positive about yourself and your capacity to learn will breed success.

The perceived cause of your success or failure in grasping new concepts/skills/knowledge or understanding the things that happen to you through your life will determine whether you operate up to the true level of your capability. In the following passages we look at optimism and self-confidence and how these can be critical in getting us to think – and act – positively in our quest to develop, grow and succeed (and remember: we are defining success as personal to each of us). But the rationalizing of why things happen or do not happen is a key starting point for us.

The underpinning factor is personal responsibility. Failing to learn to drive can be attributed to many factors, and the chart opposite indicates the kind of responses we might want to give. Taking personal responsibility – 'lack of practice', 'more engagement', 'more effort', 'listening to my instructor' – increases the chances of success. Lack of personal responsibility, where we ascribe our success or lack of it to factors outside our control – 'I'm stupid anyway', 'I was lucky', 'You caught me on a good day' – are typical comments. Here are some of the things we say when we have a conversation with ourselves – what we might call our inner dialogue.

The high-level achiever	The underachiever
I can always improve.	My level of ability is genetic.
I need to commit more time to succeed.	I can't do it.
I'll have another go.	I give up.
Confidence is good.	Confidence is arrogance.
Learn from mistakes.	Mistakes mean lack of ability.
Take responsibility.	Find excuses.
Mini success!	Beginner's luck.
What can I do?	It's my employer's fault.
I can do anything if I really try.	It's not worth the effort.

It's the ultimate self-fulfilling prophecy – believing you are capable of success dramatically increases your chances of meeting it. Low achievers can succeed in the new task but will ascribe their success to 'beginner's luck' or 'you'd have to be really stupid to not be able to do this'. Faced with lack of achievement, the underachiever denies to him/herself the possibility of ever being able to master the new task, or if he/she does succeed in a particular situation it's because of factors outside their control – anything from lack of ability through to unhelpful movements in their astrological chart.

On the other hand, faced with initial failure, high-level achievers acknowledge the opportunity for improvement through practice, hard work and so on. If we succeed, we attribute success to our endeavour – and, of course, acknowledge the work of those who have supported us.

If you don't believe you are motivated to succeed, consider this. A lifetime of underachievement requires a motivation of its own. We perform only up to the level we believe we are capable of, and it still requires motivation to perform to this level – even if it's a low level and therefore not related to your capability. The point here, to use our analogy, is that we all have our personal fire burning, but we have the choice about whether we let external factors affect its strength.

Try this exercise as a way of helping you reflect on your current level of capability and how you view your potential for the future. Write down these three column headings: 'Accomplishments', 'Capabilities' and 'Future potential'. Then, in the first column, simply list five examples of things you have accomplished. In the second column list five things you believe you are capable of, and in the third column list five things (or as many as you can) that you want to achieve.

This exercise gets really interesting when we assess what we have written, and how each column relates to the other. In 'live' sessions it is interesting how many do actually struggle to fill the five accomplishments. Did you struggle? It shouldn't be too tough, and yet some of us won't see success and achievement for what they are. Learning to drive, having a baby, decorating the house, passing an exam, learning how to use a computer, getting fit or organizing a children's party – all are accomplishments that display skills that can be used in other parts of your life. In the second column, how many of your five capabilities were provable accomplishments and how many of them were yet to be proven? Five capabilities that are provable suggest that you may be living in the past a little too much – saying, 'I'm only capable of what I have done.' You may be prone to this if you were struggling to see the difference between column one and column two.

Of course, your accomplishments may have highlighted potential future capabilities that you never knew you had or may not have even considered. Organizing a successful children's party shows many of the skills required to be a great office manager. In the early 1980s future Chicago Marathon winner Steve Jones was a 40-a-day smoker who barely moved from the sofa. An accomplishment for him was to quit smoking and start jogging – even though he didn't get much further than the bottom of the street first time out. This accomplishment threw open a huge door of future capability.

It can be helpful (though not essential) to have a link between capabilities (if they are future-focused) and future achievement because you are creating a link between you now and you future. Otherwise the future may remain just a dream. Many of us spend years developing knowledge and skills in certain areas. Think of someone who makes a decision to get fit. When we start to go to the gym regularly we begin to get a clearer view of our physical capabilities – Steve Jones would have soon realized he had to put in some serious work to get fit for the marathon! This in turn will help us to create a clearer path for future achievement in this realm – if we want it to. This could take place over many years.

To sum up, our capacity to learn and grow as people comes from four key areas:

1 The future should be an opportunity to develop new skills, not just to replay old, provable ones.
2 Setbacks and frustrations are normal. How much you let them affect you will determine how well you learn.
3 We should have a realistic view of our potential. 'I'm the greatest' (unless you are Muhammad Ali) and 'I'm hopeless' are not appropriate here.
4 (and most important of all) We should take personal responsibility.

In Chapter 5 (page 97) we look at how we go about setting goals and challenges for ourselves and in particular how our self-perception influences the setting of these goals and challenges. These four factors are important influences on the future goals we set ourselves.

Don't do yourself down

> *Sticks and stones may break my bones*
> *But words can permanently damage me.*
> Rapper on MTV

Parental influence and one-dimensional school teaching can make us believe that we are destined to fail because of a genetic inheritance or that we don't have the capabilities that our peers at school or other family members have. How often have we heard 'XYZ is the brains in the family'? And this can carry on through life. It's not surprising that some of us have such a limited view of our capability. We can remember the times at school when certain people seemed to grasp concepts and new skills quickly. The environment can be intimidating. In that environment it can be very difficult to feel positively about one's own capacity for improvement – and it's important to remember that just because one person learns quickly it does not mean they are more capable than you. Your capacity for lifelong improvement and growth is infinite. So is everybody else's.

The Introduction mentioned websites that allow you to see what old school friends are up to nowadays. What's really fascinating about these is the element of surprise at seeing that an old school acquaintance, perhaps one you'd thought had limited capabilities, has achieved much more than you ever imagined possible. At school I can remember being in awe of high achievers in sports, according them a status in my mind way above those who didn't have their sporting prowess. In my teens I was failing to appreciate the wide arc of capabilities and possibilities in life, and was limiting my estimation of 'success status' to a very narrow channel indeed. And these to my mind 'underachievers' (and yes, I probably thought them, as teenagers have a tendency to do, 'incapable') were at that stage operating in an environment not of their choosing.

Put-downs, a dull learning environment and a failure to work with the individual breed a feeling in some people that they have a fixed (usually low) level of ability. They see little scope for personal improvement. Fans of the UK television series *The Royle Family* will recall father Jim Royle constantly belittling the capabilities of his (high-potential) son Antony to the point at which Antony was likely to reflect his father's image of him. The black humour in this relationship probably came from the fact that many of us could identify with the son.

What makes this learning process harder is that one-dimensional learning methodologies – for example, teacher to class at school – may not be appropriate for some (and we can argue many) people. Many people seem to burst into life when they find an environment that suits them, or where the 'eureka' moment really hits and we realize the potential that life itself has to offer. Remember that your current competency and future capability do not need to be linked. Some realize this in life at a point at which they believe it's 'too late' to do anything about it. As we saw in Chapter 1 (page 33) Helene learnt about her great singing voice at the age of 67 and, what's more, took the chance to use it. Sadly, some never realize it. I hope by reading this book that you truly come to believe, no matter what stage of life you are at, that you can change positive thinking into positive action. You can do it now.

▓ Learning to be optimistic

We need some idea of what it might take to help us learn to really feel this most positive of emotions. Indeed, we can be positive in many arenas of life and not be inclined to be optimistic. We can see trouble ahead all the time, but choose to respond positively to these huge problems that we think are building up in front of us. There are some of us who seem to want to exist in a whirlpool of permanent crises – perhaps even creating the crises ourselves!

Although positive thinkers don't have to be optimists, it is unlikely that negative thinkers can be optimists. The belief that things can be better is not terra firma for negative thinkers because they are unlikely to see the possibility of improving their circumstances. Here are some good reasons why optimism should be home ground for us as positive thinkers.

▪ Positive thinkers combine optimism and realism. We say to ourselves, 'If I do A, B or C, I improve the chances of X, Y or Z happening.' Positive thinkers use optimism as a practical emotion, not as an act of blind faith.

▪ Optimism is more than hope: it's a near cousin (as *Emotional Intelligence* author Daniel Goleman tells us) but not the same. Those who hope may look for the armchair ride. Positive thinkers use optimism as an energizing force. Kath told us in Chapter 1 how her belief that things would get better for her as she competed in the world's most arduous alpine adventure race kept her going in the toughest moments.

▪ Both positive thinkers and optimists share a view of the world that holds possibilities as well as challenges (and how often are these the same?). The challenges can be activating for the optimist. If we believe we can overcome the challenges, we are more inclined to reach out and do just that.

■ Optimists try to deal with difficulties rather than let them overwhelm them. They believe that the extra effort required is worth it.

So you're not optimistic, and maybe past events have guided your lack of faith in the future. Can we, in spite of everything, learn to be optimistic? More than anything else it's crucial that, as positive thinkers, we recognize that our optimism is born out of our capacity to influence our own future through our thinking and actions. Here are nine actions that can help us build (this is not miraculous conversion) a more optimistic outlook.

1 How we assess what causes success or failure

We looked at this in the previous section. Let's remember that we ascribe success to ourselves. If we don't succeed, we think 'Try harder' or 'Do it differently' next time. We acknowledge the need for additional personal input even if things occur that we cannot control (which does sometimes happen). Our language needs to be positive – I 'can' rather than I 'might' succeed. And if we don't succeed, we don't automatically deduce that our chances of future success are reduced because of one disappointment.

2 Take personal responsibility

Perhaps this is the action that underpins the other eight. The help of others is a bonus and we can do much in our human relationships to bring people to our side, but ultimately it's down to us as individuals. Remember that nothing is guaranteed, but taking personal responsibility dramatically increases our chance of success.

3 Create future possibilities

Remember psychological travelling (page 45)? Use the imagination to create opportunities for yourself. Be the human search engine who widens the arc of personal exploration. If you don't look for anything, you probably won't find much.

4 Build confidence

Don't ignore your successes. Pat yourself on the back – it was you who made the difference! The more successes we have (and we really do have them all the time), the more we build our confidence. Part of the process of building confidence is a growing sense that we have a control over our own destiny.

5 Factor out 'luck'

Does luck exist? It doesn't really matter. If it does, its randomness means we can't factor it in as part of our optimistic future. 'Something will come along' is an expression of vague hope rather than a mantra of the optimistic positive thinker. Think back to Sergio's story in Chapter 1 (page 24) and how, rather than rely on luck to help him escape from his predicament, he got himself educated and entered a new world. If you believe luck doesn't exist, you are likely to believe that the positive things that happen to you come as a result of your own efforts. Perfect!

6 Feel spring in the air

During the winter pessimists see only the gloom, while optimists look forward to the coming of spring. Imagine yourself as an arable farmer who knows the opportunities spring will bring. From the sowing of seeds (positive action), the first green shoots (new energy) through to flowering and the appearance of crops (reaping our own personal harvest), the optimism pays dividends. The farmer suffers setbacks, such as late frosts, and some years the harvest isn't as good as expected; nonetheless, the 'spring' mentality is an important catalyst for the farmer – and a good learning metaphor for the positive thinker!

7 How big is the glass?

In a familiar mantra it is said that optimists see the glass half-full and pessimists see the glass half-empty. But hang on in there and don't worry if you're in the half-empty camp. Half-empty means lots of spare capacity, lots of room for manoeuvre and lots of opportunity for growth. You're maybe looking at the world from a position further back than the optimist, but that means you've got lots of scope for psychological travel and adventure.

And no one said how big the glass is!

8 Use pessimistic perspectives

We've said that optimism is not based on blind faith. Positive thinkers create positive futures because we create the conditions out of which those better futures grow. But we need to be realistic. Thinking about the things that could go wrong, the barriers, leaves us better able to deal with the difficulties when they arise, or to deal with the small problems before they get bigger. Some hard-headed realism is important. It's what drives us as positive thinkers to raise our effort level to overcome the difficulty.

A very real problem in many post-industrial societies is the number of people who get themselves into debt. Many choose to pretend that the problem will go away, or increase their spend on lottery tickets. Positive thinking in this situation requires proactive solutions – taking on extra or part-time work and so on. The initial pessimistic outlook – 'things could get really bad' – inspires positive thoughts and actions.

9 Hyperinflation

Are things as bad as you imagine them to be? The small problem that created the difficult situation gets amplified into an all-pervasive life issue to the point where you can think of little else. See things as they really are, *not* as you imagine them to be. Think about some of the problems you've had that were dragging you down in the past. Were they all as bad as you thought at the time?

Fran's story

I don't know when it really struck me, but at some point in my late teens I realized I had a particular affinity with children. It was different from what a mother has for her own children. All kinds of children seemed to be attracted to me and me to them. I had two of my own children quite young, and then, in my late twenties, my husband and I thought about being foster parents. I suppose I just had a moment of great sadness when I realized that all the love and comfort I was able to give to my own children couldn't be extended to everyone. We hear all those stories of parents abandoning their children or being abusive to them and we can only imagine what they feel. I applied to be a foster mother as an impulsive thing.

I really feel like I'm doing what I was meant to do. We all need to have some sense that our future will be good, that things can get better. For some of us it will be the wildest dreams that we try to make real. For others it might just be a yearning for love. Imagine how it must feel to be a child who doesn't know their mother and father any more. Where is the rock for them? Where is the stability? We provide that. We give them a feeling that there is good out there, that there is love. We help them see that things can be better for them. If they see things can be better, they have much to live for.

▨ Building confidence

Confidence comes from control – a sense that our thoughts and actions will have a direct and positive impact on our future. If we ask ourselves the characteristics of confident people, we might come up with a list comprising some of the following:

▨ 'Can do' mentality
Confident people are prepared to get 'stuck in' because they believe they have the capacity to succeed. This confidence generates the energy needed to do the things that will define 'success' for them.

▨ High self-esteem
Confident people have a positive (but not over-inflated) opinion of their capabilities.

▨ Intuition
Confident people intuitively feel that the direction they have chosen is a good one – even when they don't have complete information to justify the decisions they make. Perhaps they make the direction right through their own confidence and 'can do' mentality?

▨ Strong resolve
Confident people stand up for what they think is right.

▨ Confidence as an energy generator
There's nothing like believing you can do something to make you want to go out and do it.

We can balance this list by saying that confidence does not always mean success. Confidence can be misplaced through lack of realism – thinking that things will be easy or that 'something will come along'. There is also the possibility that we could become over-confident and arrogant without perhaps realizing it. Lack of realism is a subjective argument. What's unrealistic to one person may be entirely feasible to another – and they go out and prove it.

Don't let a lack of success hurt your self-esteem. There are reasons for everything. Conventional wisdom suggests that it's unacceptable to blame bad luck for a lack of success when you try something new. However, it is quite acceptable to acknowledge that there are factors outside our control. Sometimes an event can change our course, and if we want to, we can attribute our failure to bad luck. But if you do this, there are four important factors to consider:

1 Bad luck once shouldn't be a reason to not try again.

2 What we can't do is factor in the potential for good or bad luck as a reason to do or not to do something in the first place.

3 Are you certain that bad luck is not being used as a convenient excuse?

4 Success should not be attributed to luck, but to you and what you did.

These considerations play a part in building confidence. Success breeds confidence, and a critical element in the developing psyche of the positive thinker is to recognize our successes and what it was in us that made us succeed.

Self-confidence is self-raising and begins with the inner dialogue we looked at earlier that we continually have with ourselves about many of the actions we undertake. It's easy to overlook our successes because we take them for granted and don't consciously have the internal dialogue any more. Going back to the learning to drive example we used in 'Learning to learn' (page 67) – five years after passing our driving test and using highways, we think less about the success we made of learning to drive. It's interesting that those who really had to struggle to pass may be more conscious of their ultimate success even some years after the event. The depth of the struggle in any sphere of life may make us inversely more proud of our ultimate success in that sphere.

To help identify considerable areas of achievement in your own life (and thereby build your own confidence levels) draw up a simple list of things you feel you have achieved. The arena of achievement in every person's life is immense if we choose to think about it for a few minutes. Let's take parenthood as an example. Successfully raising a child is a remarkable achievement given meagre credit in North American/north European cultures (although there are signs of a backlash against this 1980s/90s culture change). Consider some of the skills involved:

Teacher	Cook	Coach	Giver of love
Guardian	Entertainer	Mentor	Time manager
Supporter	Counsellor	Enabler	Creative thinker

With that kind of success, we have a terrific basis for building self-confidence. This is just one example of the myriad successes we could have in our life, and given these successes, we are all achievers. Congratulations to you!

Building self-confidence is based on control of our personal circumstances. We accept the things we can't control, but we learn over time to control our thoughts and feelings and the impact we can have on the wider world. That is, the things we have a degree of control over. Harold Macmillan, British Prime Minister from 1957 to 1963, once remarked that the only things he lost sleep over were 'events, dear boy, events'. But even with unexpected events, if we wanted any proof of our capacity to respond to them in remarkable ways, we need only look at the human response (positive and immediate, individual rather than political) to the late 2004 Asian tsunami disaster. Many of us in crises throw self-doubt out of the window and recognize the need to get on with it.

Here are some reminders to help you build your own confidence.

▓ Don't be impatient

We are unlikely to switch from lacking confidence to being highly confident in a few days, although sometimes this can happen. Instead, confidence is more likely to build incrementally over time. It can help to think about something you are good at now and work back over the stages you went through to get to the point at which you are today. Try this in reverse. Pick a point in the future where you are succeeding in something at which you currently lack confidence. What were the things that helped to build your confidence to the point at which you are succeeding? Try to work those confidence-building measures and actions into your current life.

A good example where this can work for us comes in something many people fear – making presentations. Even after a little training or coaching, it is unrealistic for most of us to expect to be the next Martin Luther King or Winston Churchill. Regular practice and feedback will help us reach a level of competence in the short term, and over time we can work to improve.

■ Bounce back

The path to being a more positive, confident person is not smooth. Setbacks come along to test the most confident of people. Failing to pass your driving test, not getting that promotion, or losing in a sporting contest are all typical experiences that can test our confidence levels. Confident people learn from these experiences and from mistakes that they may have made, but they don't let them diminish their own self-belief. A mistake-free life means a life lived without trying anything new. The setback or the mistake is often much less important than the reaction to it. Understanding that there will be setbacks and that we all experience them helps us to keep perspective and make sure that the setback doesn't unduly affect our confidence.

Inventor Sir Clive Sinclair, who popularized the pocket calculator, was once asked about all the failures he had had as an inventor – some readers will recall the Sinclair C5 car! Sir Clive gave two responses. The first was that he couldn't have had the successes without the failures. Success is never guaranteed, but not trying because of fear of failure guarantees no success. The second was that the successes made the failures worth while – the failures were an essential part of being successful.

In a similar vein Thomas Edison learnt a thousand ways *not* to make a lightbulb before he eventually found a way to make one.

■ Inner mind...out-of-body experiences

We have the capacity to think into our future. We visualize things that may happen to us in the future such as making a presentation, confronting a difficult issue with a colleague or even performing at a sports event. We mentally rehearse what will happen by visualizing ourselves in that position. We create alternative scenarios – 'What would I do if this happens?' and so on. This mental rehearsal helps build confidence in our capacity to deal with challenging situations and setbacks that occur along the way.

■ Learn to be assertive

Our work is one aspect of our life where we can find it difficult to express ourselves assertively. Unnecessary demands, the pressure to socialize and the aggression of others towards us can be stressful if we don't have the confidence to assert ourselves. Think of those times in the office when someone asked you to do something and you really could not do it through lack of time. How often did you say 'yes' when you had the right to say 'no' – or fail to provide an alternative solution?

Being assertive is rooted in our being able to express what we want, need, think or feel directly in an open, honest manner that respects the rights of those with whom we come into contact. Being assertive means standing up for ourselves when others are seeking to force their own views on us. We must not, however, confuse our capacity for being assertive with aggressive behaviour. And at the other end of the spectrum being passive ensures we get trodden on for years to come.

■ Build positive relationships

You can't always choose the people around you but you can choose your attitude to them. In Chapter2 (Travelling to other worlds) we talked about the value of proactive listening and getting into the mind of others so that you can understand them better and what they are saying to you.

Another great way to build positive relationships based on honesty and mutual benefit is to be able to give and receive feedback to and from others. If we can receive feedback we get a clear steer on what we are doing well and where we can improve.

■ Accentuate success

In the real world many of us are confident in certain aspects of our life but sometimes lack confidence in others. Perhaps you're confident at work but your relationships outside that area don't pan out. Or you are a successful captain of a sports team but struggle to be effective as a manager at work.

Focus on the positive and let your confident self rather than your unconfident self permeate your wider thinking. Look back at your achievements in the 'Learning to learn' section (page 67) and remind yourself of them.

■ **Brand 'me'**

Imagine you are a marketing manager and you want to sell the brand 'you' to the general public. What can you say about 'you'? Be the person that you want yourself to be. Pick some words from those listed below that sell you in the best way possible, and then be that person. How many of these descriptions fit with you? What other words would you use?

trusting	positive	energetic	intuitive
caring	optimistic	risk-taking	optimistic
committed	highly capable	confident	supportive
creative	assertive	challenging	organized

You could experiment with someone you personally admire – parent, friend, musician, politician. Think about the qualities that make them what they are. Would you like some of those qualities to apply to you?

> *Why not build your own personal 'mission statement ' – give yourself something to work towards?*

In this chapter we have worked with a series of mental tools – opportunity-spotting, learning to learn and to be optimistic, building confidence – that will help to fan our inner flame so that it becomes a beautiful roaring fire. But not a fire that gets out of control!

These mental tools will work better if used in conjunction with the growing self-awareness that is the theme of the next chapter. Here we will dig a little deeper and begin to 'tune into' ourselves.

There's a person I know,
a person I can go to,
and s/he's living deep
inside me…

Chapter 4
Tuning in

❏ Knowing me

❏ Making intuition work

❏ Whole…heart…head…ness

In the days when radios needed to be manually tuned in, we had to move the tuning dial a little bit to the left or a little bit to the right until we got the station we wanted to listen to as clearly as we could.

It's a bit like that when we try to tune into ourselves – when we try to understand what makes us tick at a deeper level. We can spend a lifetime attempting to tune into radio station 'me' and never finding it, or not listening when we have connected. We all continually talk to ourselves in our head. This 'other person' you talk to is a great friend. Get to know them a little better by tuning into the wavelength that is your best ally – and listen.

■ Knowing me

Understanding our innermost self takes a combination of desire, time and honesty. It requires us to have 'experiences' and to consider subsequently how we reacted to those experiences. We also need to consider that our reactions in one situation may not be the same as our reactions in another. Remember some of the points we looked at in the last chapter about building confidence and improving our learning skills. We may feel confident enough in one aspect of our life that comes easily to us – social skills, for example – but in another aspect – say, making presentations – we recognize the need for extra effort to get us up to the required standard. This isn't just a confidence issue – it's a reality check. The confidence issue, however, is important because confidence is not just about our belief in our ability to do something; it's also about our belief in our capacity to *learn* to do something.

Positive thinking helps us to believe that we are capable of doing many things, but it also helps us to believe that, through our own efforts, we can improve our knowledge and skills. And isn't it a delicious feeling to find ourselves performing beyond the level we initially believed we were capable of because we put in the hard work required early enough! However, what is critical here is that this person (and I hope it happens to you) knows him- or herself well enough to be able to recognize the need to learn and to believe that they have the capacity to do this.

Deep down most of us recognize character traits in ourselves that we learn through experience to nurture, control and make use of if we can in practical applications. In its most evangelical form, positive-thinking gurus tell us to shut out the genetic 'character trait' inheritance, or even, at its most extreme, that this genetic inheritance does not exist at all. This is nonsense. As positive thinkers we need to understand our natural inclinations and preferences as well as our strengths and weaknesses. Where positive thinking pays dividends is in our belief that we can:

- Turn weaknesses into strengths
- Nurture and feed our strengths
- Learn to control our emotions
- Adapt our behaviour to suit the situation

Remember Sergio, who said that one of the skills of the survivor he'd identified was the individual's ability to make an honest appraisal of his or her strengths and weaknesses (see page 25).

Understanding me

How do I think, act, feel, believe and behave? These are very big questions to answer but we can take a little from Helene's story in Chapter 1 (page 33). Helene learnt to challenge her self-perception and discovered that while she had thought she was shy and introverted, she was actually extroverted. Her self-perception had significantly held her back up to that point.

To understand yourself a little better, it can be a useful exercise to write down a few personality traits that you perceive in yourself and then to recall times when your thinking and/or behaviour contradicted this self-perception. If there are lots of examples, your self-perception may be wrong. And even if your behaviour so far reflects your self-perception, you may be behaving a certain way only because you think you are that way.

Of course, you might be very happy with you the way you are! If your religion is your guide, this will influence your actions, feelings and beliefs. Or it could be that you are comfortable with the personality coat that you wear now.

Controlling myself

How do I control my thoughts, feelings, impulses and behaviour? This requires a substantial degree of honesty. Do you seek conflict and argument? Do you fly off the handle a little too quickly and create more problems than you solve, or do you generally remain in control even in challenging situations?

Self-control can be difficult to exercise when we get frustrated with others who don't see things our way or perhaps aren't grasping things as quickly as we had hoped – at work perhaps. It can also be tough to retain self-control when we feel that we are losing control of our circumstances. It's that loss of self-control that may be creating those circumstances for us.

Impulses can be good – they help create much-needed spontaneity in our life. But impulsive actions can also damage relationships. Sometimes it pays to think. Think of the out-of-control sports person – soccer players attacking referees, for example – whose impulses hijacked their reason.

Motivating myself

How easy do I find it to drive myself to perform tasks, learn new skills or even get out of bed in the morning? Now might be a good time to look at some of those exercises in 'Opportunity knocks' (page 61) and 'Learning to learn' (page 67) and to ask how strongly the internal flame is currently burning.

Projecting myself

How do I see the future? Do I let past experiences control future possibilities?

It's understandable that we let past experiences affect our perception of the future. Previous successes – a salesperson who sells lots of product or a champion athlete – will use those past successes to build up the confidence bank account for use in the future.

It's where past mistakes and failures are reducing the potential that the future has to offer that we need to be aware. Are you setting your sights too low because of things that have happened in the past? And are you discount-ing the positive impact your own actions can have on your future?

Gavin's story in Chapter 1 has a resonance here because despite a near-death experience on Everest, his appetite for adventure remains undiminished. His survival reaffirmed his belief in himself and what he does. Others might have decided never even to look at a mountain again.

Do you believe you can think and act in a more positive way even if your life so far makes it difficult for you to do so?

■ Making intuition work

If we seek complete information to make decisions, it is likely that we will never have enough facts to reach any decision at all. We become paralysed by the need to know more before we make the leap. Positive thinkers often have very little to go on when making decisions about their own future, but are prepared to back their intuition. Intuition provides us with a kind of sensory osmosis that eases us into the future. Think how important intuition must have been to Anita Roddick or Richard Branson when they started businesses with very little to back them other than a gut feeling that their decision was the right one. Or, on a smaller scale, someone who runs one of those highly successful quirky shops in small towns when logic says there would be no market for what they sell.

In the Western world, however, fact after fact is demanded on which to make decisions – a process that has the only partially hidden adjunct saying that if I made the wrong decision, it wasn't my fault, it was the fault of the facts! It may be that we are preparing the excuses for making the wrong decision before we've actually made it.

This admittedly cynical view does not, however, undermine the amount we use our intuition when making decisions. In many situations we will combine rational, logical processes with our intuition to try to reach the 'right' answer. A classic example is in the development of a relationship. In such a case we intuit all the time. We often tell ourselves to what degree we are attracted to someone fairly early in the process of getting to know that person. It may be on the basis of 'feel' – something fits with them (intuitive) – or it may be that we say we like people with certain physical characteristics (rational). What gets us past the initial day or so of what might be a temporary fancy is, however, often an intuitive feel that someone is right for us – even if they don't fit the stereotype of the person we thought we might be with long term. It may explain why those who have pre-set ideas about the type of person they want to be with may end up lonely.

The advent of speed dating and other dating rituals demonstrates the attempt to short-circuit that other key element in establishing a relationship – time. The busy person who doesn't have the time to 'get to know someone' or to 'meet new people' decides to rely on a few facts to get the process started. Despite the publicity given to the people who meet their life partner in this way, the success rate is very low. The process of attraction is frequently not a matching of likes and interests – and there is increasing evidence to suggest that opposites *do* attract. There are far more subtle processes at play, linking personality, experience, hormones, need – even smell, apparently!

Gut feeling and intuition often guide us in these situations, with little recourse to rational, deliberative thought processes. Intuition is a core element in the psyche of the positive thinker too. But using intuition means entering into a world of uncertainty, of emotion, of instinct, and for some that is an uncomfortable prospect.

Is it possible, then, for us to develop our intuition so that we are able to make better decisions? Perhaps the biggest difficulty is that it is a subject that is still not taken entirely seriously. Some see it as woolly decision-making. Try to justify the next significant decision you make at work on the basis that it 'feels right'. Although some business leaders cite intuition as a guiding light, the majority do not. And shareholders definitely won't! Before making a decision, the intuitive person tunes into feelings as well as acknowledging facts, while the rational, logical thinker accumulates evidence.

So what is intuition? It is a subject that frustrates psychologists and scientists alike because they are unable to define it specifically and cannot therefore give us the X number of laws of intuitive thinking. It is an emotional mechanism that we have yet to really understand, and it may be that once we know what it is and how it works, it ceases to be intuition anyway. It could be a subject that is always one step away from mastery. Perhaps that is what makes it so interesting.

If this is a little deflating for positive-thinking readers who want clear guidance here, it needn't be. Positive thinkers need to respond to ambiguity and uncertainty, and it seems that it might be possible to fine-tune our intuition. Here are some interesting pointers to help us get a little nearer to understanding how our intuition might work.

■ Intuition gives us the umbrella view of a situation when we are stuck in the minutiae of detail.

■ When we try to use intuition part of us goes into silent mode because we clear out the facts from our conscious thinking.

■ When we start being judgemental we are no longer using intuition.

■ Intuition cannot tell the time. Sometimes it's quick and sometimes it's slow. We can't always control its pace.

■ Intuition is the residue left over when all of our psychological baggage has been removed.

Intuition is often said to work for at least some of the following reasons (the language used here will be familiar to readers who have read some of the other sections in this and other chapters):

■ We pay attention to the times when intuition seems to work. It could be that it works because we own the solution deeply and are more positively committed to it. Or it could be that we blame factors other than failed intuition when it doesn't.

■ Intuitive decisions are a reflection of me inside myself. The solution is the best for me and the kind of person I am – that's why it feels right. If it feels right, I am likely to be more committed to action.

■ Use of intuition can be a positive, confidence-building action because we are telling ourselves that we actually know more than we think we know: 'I have this other person who helps me out.' Having confidence that we can get it right makes us strive to do exactly that.

■ In reality we often combine both intuition and logical, rational thinking processes, so it is difficult to attribute success to just one or the other (refer to the later section on 'Whole...heart...head...ness', page 93). Einstein openly stated that he used both.

Can we access our intuition when we need it? It may be that our intuition works best when we are truly emotionally engaged – when we really care about something. If we don't care enough, we don't dial the numbers to our intuition. So how can we connect to it?

■ For the most part we connect better with our intuition when we shut out noise, thinking and other people. If you are pondering a particular challenge or problem and have a course of action in mind, shut your mind off for a few moments and the residual feeling that you have could be your intuition telling you whether the action is wise or not.

■ While you are grappling with a problem and shutting off outside influences, try closing your eyes and hiding each possible solution behind something like an imaginary door. Then imagine which is the easiest door to open – this can help to provide direction.

■ It seems that the brain can switch modes from logical and reasoning to intuitive and back again. A number of scientists report a connection (intuitive) to a solution when making new discoveries long before the evidence (logic, reason) supported their view. Readers who want to learn more about this will find Guy Claxton's *Hare Brain, Tortoise Mind* a stimulating read.

■ We find our intuition more easily if we make a long-term commitment to improve it – a notion that we are now going to look at further.

Positively preparing to use intuition

Guy Claxton rightly suggests that referring to the infallibility of intuition takes an inflated view of its power, and he cites the *Chambers Dictionary* definition – 'the power of the mind by which it immediately perceives *the truth* [my italics] of things without reasoning or analysis' – as an example of the overstated view of intuition. This assumes that intuition always works – which it doesn't.

During the world chess championship between Gary Kasparov and Nigel Short in 1993 both players talked about the 'truth' of the position. This is the point at which chess players are able to intuitively see the complete reality (the 'truth') of the position in front of them. They have to because in a game there just isn't the time to work through millions of move permutations. The fingers (connected to one's intuition) are playing the pieces on the board and the better fingers will normally win. Chess is a game where the 'truth' of the position of the pieces on the board may become apparent only years later. It is interesting that even in a game whose *raison d'être* sometimes seems to be post-game analysis rather than the game itself, intuitive 'feel' for the state of play has to override mechanical thinking processes.

It is almost as though the rigorous analysis of millions of chess game permutations is a preparation for the use of intuition in a real match. Perhaps here lies a clue for positive thinkers who want to sharpen their decision-making skills by using intuition. Can we prepare ourselves to be more intuitive? Furthermore, can we through practice, experience, 'scenario planning' and so on prepare ourselves for a time or times when we need our intuition to work for us? The answer, if we follow the example of chess players, is a very cautious 'yes'!

Hoping for something

There is a view that says that either our intuition is always right (if it is wrong, you weren't using your intuition correctly) or that it doesn't exist. Perhaps the real difficulty is that an intuitive feeling that something was right initially leads us to single-mindedly pursue a particular course of action during which time the goal-posts shift and our initial intuitive feeling is no longer right, or we acknowledge the fact that sometimes our intuition is wrong. We can think of times when we were convinced of something without a logical reason for being so, took off in a particular direction and found our initial feeling to be wrong. Perhaps as positive thinkers we need to recognize what is an intuitive feeling and what is 'fool's hope'.

I myself, in a period of my life when I enjoyed horse-racing a little too much, can remember convincing myself that a horse called Flown was going to win the Cheltenham Champion Hurdle, a major British horse race, to the point where I placed a series of ante-post bets on it to do just that. I thought I instinctively felt it was going to win. What I was doing was irrationally hoping it was going to win. It didn't win!

Irrational hope is not the same as intuition.

■ Whole…heart…head…ness

In the last section on intuition we looked at emotion-based, intuitive 'thinking' together with more logical, rational processes. What seems clear, however, is that we need both. The chess players we discussed do not really play without consciously thinking, and those who survive purely on emotional reactions and feelings could end up as emotional wrecks. In reality, we do not use only one process or the other in generating solutions and making decisions. As futurologist Joel Barker tells us:

> **Intuitive judgement: it is the ability to make good decisions with incomplete data.**

But not often, it has to be said, with no data.

Intuition is just one element of emotion-based response. What we can argue here is that positive thinkers commit to ideas and decisions through the engagement of both the emotional and the rational, reasoning elements of our psyche. Through practice and experience we can learn how much of each is required. We have used the example of learning to drive before, and it is a useful example again here. If and when you learnt to drive, on what basis did you make that decision? Some of the reasons may have been rational and logical – particularly if you learnt a little later in life. These reasons could be:

- I need to drive for my work.
- I've had enough of bad public transport.
- I need to get around quickly.

Other reasons may have been more emotion-based:

- It gives me a sense of freedom.
- I like cars.
- I have a feeling that I might need it.

If we commit to new personal initiatives, such as learning to drive or taking up jogging, it can pay to wholly commit rather than to engage only part of ourselves. For example, if we've taken up jogging to get ourselves fit, there will always be days when we don't particularly feel like it. In those situations our head will tell us to get out there because it's good for us. Our more emotional side will start building up the guilt feelings at our own lethargy. We often find that as we weigh up the reasons to learn a new skill or develop one that has been treading water for a while, we secure our own emotional commitment to the whole process. If we are 'half-hearted' about something – that is to say, we are only partially emotionally engaged – we shouldn't be surprised if we don't succeed. Similarly, if we haven't produced good reasons (i.e. have been less than 'whole-headed') for doing something, but we proceed anyway, we may find ourselves directionless. So a 'whole…heart…head' approach may be best for positive thinkers. But, and this is a big but, we should not discount the possibilities inherent in being just 'whole-hearted' – where the decision is intuitive and emotion-based. Risk-takers live in this world and sometimes their risk-taking is fully justified by the results. At other times the results don't justify the decision. What we can say for certain is that being less than wholehearted when taking risks can be a recipe for failure.

The emotional side of us gives us the desire to act. The rational side gives us the reasons. They can, however, feed off each other. We motivate ourselves to do something because we can see good reasons for doing it. Or we get a gut feeling that a previously unthought-of course of action would be good and we seek reasons to justify taking that course of action. If the head were all-powerful, logic says that none of us would smoke cigarettes. Giving up probably requires an overarching amount of emotional desire to do just that. The logical reasons to give up are conclusive, but we need a lot of heart to do it. Of course 'whole...heart...head...ness' is best, but heart alone can get you a long way.

In this chapter we've looked at the deeper emotional side of ourselves and how it plays such an important part in us as positive thinkers. Tuning into our deeper feelings – where we learn to understand how we think, feel, intuit, believe – can help us make the decisions that are right for us as individuals. The more we learn to listen to ourselves, the better able we are to 'feel' our way into a more positive future. If we make choices and decisions that are right for us we automatically secure our commitment to making those choices and decisions work for us. A heart-felt engagement with our future helps to give us personal 'ownership' of that future.

If one does not know to which port one is sailing, no wind is favourable.

Seneca, Roman philosopher

Chapter 5
Go where you want to go

❏ Herding GOATs

❏ No GOATs

❏ SMARTER GOATs

❏ Ten tips for looking after the GOATs

W e need direction in our lives. Without it, many of our actions may end up having little clear purpose. Think of those times when you had something to aim for – passing an exam, passing your driving test, buying a house, moving abroad – and how much focus that gave to your actions. Or think of athletes, even those who run for fun, and how important it is to them to monitor their speed, aim for a personal best and, for those at the top, to win medals at national and international meetings.

It's at such times that we need GOATs!

G   Goal
O   Objective
A   Aim
T   Target

To me, goals, objectives, aims and targets are almost the same thing – readers will have their own favourite words – but perhaps the acronym GOAT will lodge memorably in the mind.

GOAT-setting can be important for positive thinkers because it can provide a channel for all the positive thoughts going though our heads. But it can be a catalyst for positive thoughts too. If we begin to see the possibility of our aspirations made real through effective GOAT-setting, we are likely to become energized and optimistic about our future.

But even at this early stage it's important to stress that we can be positive thinkers and have almost no GOATs at all. We can be confident, optimistic opportunity-spotters but not feel the need to be putting short-, medium- or long-term GOATs in front of ourselves. We explore this a little further in this chapter.

■ Herding GOATs

Our GOATs are rarely achieved by moving in straight lines. We can think of the journey to realize our GOATs as being a bit like negotiating the strands of a spider's web in the top corner of your bedroom. A few of the strands are broken, there are some obstacles, but there is a clear centre. To get to the centre we need to move around the web, negotiating the obstacles, moving right or left rather than straight ahead, but in little doubt as to the ultimate direction.

Returning to our GOAT theme, we often find ourselves 'herding' – keeping the GOATs together, keeping them headed in the right direction. Herders of animals work in open pasture. This open pasture – the arena of life – offers opportunities but also great challenges: plenty of space in which to give our GOATs freedom but also plenty of room for them to run off.

But let's add a little here. What happens if you've got four or five of these GOATs running around that refuse to be herded? We can't give one a disproportionate amount of time because the others will go off in another direction. We soon lose control. Our GOATs conflict, overlap and compete for our time.

A simple exercise is to do a little personal scenario-planning. When we scenario-plan we think about what possible events could interrupt us as we try to attain our GOATs. Imagine some different scenarios and ask yourself how you might cope if X or Y happened. If things don't go as planned, we find ourselves better able to adapt because we've prepared the scenario in our mind.

It is a curiosity of North American/north European societies that they take a 'one way to achieve our goal' approach. In Latin countries the approach may be more laid back, but people from these cultures often have a more fluid approach to achieving goals: they recognize that there may be more than one way of doing soomething, so they often implement several different approaches. What seems like chaos to the highly organized Westerner is actually a very effective way of responding to difficulties when they hit – as they surely will. Latin people can change tack quickly (and with less stress) because they've thought of many different ways of getting from A to B. The secret is to allow for the possibility of different future scenarios, as well as the possible implementation of a number of different approaches.

GOAT control: some tips

■ Life's path is rarely smooth – life doesn't roll out the red carpet for us. Injecting realism by being prepared for the downs helps us to deal with them. Expect the unexpected.

■ Obstacles and challenges are inevitable. If we believe we can overcome them, we are already halfway to doing just that.

■ Anticipate future events – what could happen?

■ Sometimes the sand shifts. The goal that was a great idea last year has ceased to be needed or relevant this year.

■ Keep adaptable. The carefully planned strategy may need to be changed to reflect a changing situation.

■ Beware of 'only one solution' thinking.

■ No GOATs

> *It's only when we truly know and understand that we have a limited time on Earth – and that we have no way of knowing when our time is up – that we begin to live each day to the fullest, as if it were the only one we had.*
>
> Elizabeth Kubler-Ross

Elizabeth Kubler-Ross became the world's leading thinker in helping people cope with serious change in their life. Often this meant bereavement. I discovered the above quote two days after she died, which gave it an extra poignancy. This great quote has so much impact when we consider how many people she must have seen nearing the end or at the end of their life who'd realized that every day was very special.

Living in the moment and enjoying the spontaneity that life has to offer can be just as rewarding as the achievement of longer-term aspirations. Sometimes, even with all this goal-setting, we need just to get out there and do it and, as suggested earlier in this chapter, it is perfectly possible to be a positive thinker and have no GOATs at all. Too many GOATs can be distracting for us if we cease to be able to access the pleasure of 'being in the moment'. Too much future focus and we miss what's around us now. There can be little point in going for the big goals if we neglect the things that can give us pleasure now.

Sometimes it can be healthy to try new things without having a preconceived idea of where they may take you. We see examples of the positive side of no clear end goal in two of the stars in Chapter 1. Our adventurer Gavin says that he often doesn't see a new project as 'a goal, more as an adventure'. He sometimes finds it productive to try new things to see where they take him. Helene learnt to sing at 67 with little idea about where it would take her – she had vague notions of maybe joining a church choir. As we know from her story, she now travels the world with the London Philharmonic. Both Gavin and Helene were committed to what they were doing, but didn't need the specific goal to secure their commitment.

A fixation on 'purpose' can be restrictive because we allow little room for experimentation. Sometimes it can pay to have a go, and all the great positive thinking traits – optimism, learning new skills, spotting opportunities, building confidence – work equally well if we are living a more spontaneous existence. Think about deciding to get fit by taking up jogging. Maybe we want to get fit just because it makes us feel good. Or maybe we've taken the decision because we've entered the local road race.

One way of looking at this appears in 'Knowing Me' (page 86). Are you the kind of person who likes specific goals or do you prefer to live on the hoof? Or perhaps, like many others, you need some of both?

Captured moments of spontaneity can be far more valuable than the rigidly planned pursuit of personal goals.

▓ SMARTER GOATs

In the early 1950s business thinker Peter Drucker came up with the SMART acronym to help businesses set effective objectives, and it soon became the gold standard for effective GOAT-setting. SMART gained two new elements to become SMARTER, and began to be used to help individuals set effective GOATs for themselves. SMARTER can work because it is highly logical and helps simplify what can be a tough process for many of us. SMARTER goes like this:

S Specific
M Measurable
A Action-based
R Realistic
T Timed
E Energizing
R Reviewed

Variations have included the 'A' standing for 'Agreed' – this is important in a situation where you are working as part of a team or perhaps with one other colleague. Critics suggest that there needs to be scope for GOATs to be challenging. We suggest that a GOAT will be Energizing only if it is challenging. GOATs that don't stretch us more than a little are unlikely to excite us and create a desire for action.

Before we work through SMARTER we need to be clear on purpose. Think back to your school days when many of your schoolmates (and maybe you too!) were asking the maths teacher what was the point of learning any more about the subject when we could see little need to go beyond basic arithmetic and fractions. Failure to create a purpose on the teacher's part resulted in disengagement for many. The wall that was maths for many of us became mystifying because no need was created to climb the wall.

Asking and being able to answer the 'why' question gives us the extra impetus for action. It creates the purpose.

As we work through SMARTER, we will give some examples of using it when going after a short-term and a long-term goal. The short-term goal is to complete the local 10-km (6-mile) road race that takes place in four months' time. (We're assuming our runner hasn't done a lot of running recently!) The second is a much bigger long-term goal – a person is seeking to really stretch himself or herself by attempting to learn to speak Chinese. I've chosen this example (and it could be any language) because with the changes we will see in the world economy in the next decade this could become very real for a number of the more enterprising readers of this book. And, as we know, positive thinkers are great opportunity-spotters!

So what is our purpose here? Saying 'I want to learn some languages' is a helpful first step, and 'I'm going to learn Chinese' is a useful second one, but things get a lot more interesting when we define the purpose as 'I want to make the most of future employment opportunities in the world's fastest-growing economy'. An energizing statement for many of us. For the runner, at this stage it is simply to complete the road race.

Specific

Successful GOAT-setters take practical ideas, inspirational thoughts and even dreams and turn them into tangible realities. We do this by being specific about what it is we want to achieve. 'To be able to speak Chinese with a Chinese person for five minutes' is much more motivating than saying 'To have some Chinese lessons'. It may, however, be possible that what captured our imagination in the first place was a spontaneous decision to have a few lessons to see how we found the language.

Measurable

The old saying goes that 'What gets measured gets done'. Our runner has a clear measure – to complete the race – but over time it may be that our runner will get a better idea of their level of capability and will seek to complete the race in a particular time.

We should try to build in measures where we can. In the case of our person learning to speak Chinese, perhaps there is a qualification they could obtain that would provide a useful measure. Five years is a long-term goal, and our Chinese speaker would need to set milestones on the way to monitor progress.

Don't get too hung up on the measurables, though. It can be counter-productive to enforce measurables artificially when sometimes we just don't need to. There are some things that should not be measured – humour and attitude, for example!

Action-based

Action is that crucial link between the desire to do something and the doing. Positive action words like 'increase' or 'improve' or 'complete' work better than vague 'try to', 'have a look at' statements. 'Register for the course' is a proactive action-based statement.

Realistic

We have already observed that one person's realism is another person's fantasy, and in some situations this will be a highly subjective judgement. Try to stand back a little and take the 'helicopter view' by looking over the whole situation rather than getting stuck in smaller parts of it – ask if what we are seeking to do is realistic. Our runner may find it helpful to go out jogging a few times to assess their current capability. Our Chinese learner may find it useful to have a few exploratory lessons first or to talk with the tutor to see what GOAT would be realistic. Past experiences may help us assess what is possible in the future too. There is a fine dividing line between what is challenging and what is unrealistic. We need the challenging part. A lack of realism will frustrate us and cause us to have an earlier than planned review.

Timed

By when? Our motivated language-learner is looking to speak to a certain standard in five years – a clear deadline. Sometimes with long-term GOATs we need the end deadline and some milestones along the way to help check we're making progress. Sometimes, however, it might just be that although we have the end goal, we may have no realistic basis on which to give an end deadline. In this situation the milestones become even more important.

Energizing

SMARTER theory says that by fulfilling the SMARTER criteria we will be creating a desire to achieve because we are expressing the idea, aspiration or dream in such a way that we can see it becoming real. This sense of bringing the future to us excites us and drives us towards achieving it.

At its best, SMARTER creates clear direction for vague aspirations, but there are times when it can fail to be energizing. Many readers will have come across SMART or its successor SMARTER through the annual appraisal or performance review at their workplace. As laudable as the original intention may have been, the appraisal process has become much derided and is often seen to fail because the whole process is often 'owned' by a third party – usually Personnel or Human Resources (we are human beings, not human resources!). Both parties, appraiser and appraisee, feel they are jumping through the hoops for the benefit of someone else and do not input to the process in a 'whole…heart…head' way. We have to engage when we set our goals. Doing it because someone else says we have to or because we have a vague feeling that it might be a good idea is not a great way to secure our commitment. If we don't really 'feel' it, no amount of SMARTER will make it happen for us.

Children (and this applies to many adults too) do not really have many clear objectives in their life. When asked why they are doing particular things, many will reply, 'Because I have to'. This failure to link actions with need or purpose can lead to a lack of desire in adulthood. Children are often curious enough to want to know more, but we cannot abuse this curiosity for too long. Eventually children want reasons to justify their actions. This process of asking ourselves why we are undertaking particular actions or tasks is important for many of us. Successfully answering the 'why' can create an energizing purpose in our lives.

Reviewed

Regularly review progress. We should ask ourselves how we are getting along. Often we will have a gut feeling about the progress we are making. At other times we will know because we have or haven't reached the milestones we have set.

In the second exercise in the Personal resources section (page 182) there's a chart that you can use as a model to help you set your own SMARTER GOATs. It has worked examples based on the runner and the learner of Chinese whom we mentioned earlier. After reading these, why not draw up your own chart, adding relevant details under each heading?

■ Ten tips for looking after the GOATs

1 Create milestones

When we work towards some of our bigger GOATs, we sometimes need to create milestones to help us check the rightness of the direction. In this situation it can be a good idea to try to set the GOAT and then work through the milestones with someone who is able to add a reality check – in the case of the example we used in the SMARTER GOATs section, learning to speak Chinese, it could be a teacher. Say, for example, we set a SMARTER target – 'In five years' time I will be able to have a conversation with a Chinese person for five minutes' – and we've given the purpose, 'so that I can make the most of job opportunities in the world's fastest-growing economy', we may want to set a few personal milestones along the way.

Overleaf is an example of how this might work. Try it with one of your own bigger GOATs.

After one year – To have learnt the alphabet and be able to enunciate the letters

After two years – To be able to repeat basic questions in Chinese: 'What is your name?', 'How old are you?' and 'Where do you live?' First visit to China to get a feel for the people and their culture

After three years – To be able to structure sentences

After four years – To be able to put a number of sentences together

After five years – To reach my goal of speaking with a Chinese person for five minutes in Chinese

When we do this we get a clear indication of whether we are on the right path to the attainment of our bigger GOAT. Play a little with the milestones until you feel comfortable that you have got them right. But remember that each milestone needs to be challenging.

There is no reason why this process couldn't work for smaller, short-term GOATs too. How might our jogger approach this?

After one month – To be able to run for 30 minutes every day without stopping

After two months – To increase the daily run to 45 minutes

After three months – To be running an hour a day. To begin to consider the time target I might want to set in the race

After three months and two weeks – To be running for one hour at the pace at which I want to run in the race itself

Two days before – To rest the body before the race itself

Of course, our milestones are mini-GOATs themselves. Whatever kinds of GOAT we set, we must recognize the need sometimes to change the GOAT. It might be that our runner will be satisfied with completion of the race in any kind of time, so the issue of pace is taken out of the equation. Or our Chinese learner realizes that progress is bit quicker than expected and the GOAT becomes a four-year rather than a five-year one.

When we set GOATs for ourselves, milestones help to monitor our progress in achieving the bigger GOAT.

2 Have more first-time experiences

Don't let fear of the unknown stop you taking on new challenges.

Part of the reason, it is said, that life seems to speed up as we get older is that as we progress through adulthood into the third age we have less 'first-time', memorable experiences that get lodged in the conscious memory bank. Seeking novelty is an essential part of us and yet we feel more comfortable operating in familiar territory. Living a repetitive life brings, inevitably, little variety. It's that lack of variety that can lead to mental and physical stagnation. We tend to remember little if there is little to remember. It seems likely that routine living, devoid of variety, doesn't disappear from the memory bank altogether, but gets stored in the deeper recesses of the unconscious state, where it's harder to access. The memorable experience gets lodged closer to the most accessible parts of our brain.

We lose our conscious memory if there's nothing worth remembering.

Does the memory decline as we get older because our brain is slowly dying or because we have less in our life that is memorable? The answer is likely to be a combination of the two. We can't do much about the ageing process (yet!) but we can do something about feeding our desire for novelty and variety.

And do remember, as we said earlier in this chapter, that sometimes it can be healthy not to have GOATs at all! The psychological traveller (see Chapter 2, page 45) will find a million and one things in the world to enjoy. There's nothing wrong with dipping your toe in the water – perhaps a little creative experimentation to find out what's there. We need to be careful not to be so blinded by the big life GOATs that we forget to try new things. Who knows, the little things now might turn into the big GOATs of the future.

I don't want fame to limit me from having new experiences.
Leonardo DiCaprio

Leonardo DiCaprio's comment is a great one. There is probably little doubt that he is doing exactly what he wants to vocationally, but even then he sees himself as the human search engine – looking, as he says, for 'new experiences'. What we are not talking about here is sampling new things for the sake of them. In my late teenage years I was intrigued by Inter-railers, who took the opportunity to travel around Europe by rail for a month on a cheap rail pass. Some seemed to spend most of the month looking at the world from a train carriage, perhaps stopping at certain cities only for a day – almost, it seemed, so that they could say, 'I've been there'. They appeared to have little real engagement with the places they visited. Others of course engaged 'whole...heart...head...ly' with their surroundings and had a richer experience as a result. It was Oscar Wilde who said that 'too much foreign travel can dull the mind'. Particularly the mind that isn't curious about the destination.

Don't take opportunity for granted.

Many of us will have observed that the person who seems to have a balanced approach to their work – unstressed, productive and so on – also seems to have worked plenty of new experiences into their non-work existence. Maybe their vocation and vacation merge into one seamless expression of living? (See Chapter 7, 'Playing for a living'.)

Remember that great saying, 'When was the last time you did something for the first time?' And remember Helene in Chapter 1 who did something for the first time – learning to sing – and where that took her.

3 Generate stretch GOATs

Not every GOAT needs to be highly challenging, but personal fulfilment may be reached only if we have at least one or two stretching GOATs in our life that challenge our existing capabilities and help us in the development of new ones.

The stretch GOAT will be related to what we perceive our capabilities to be and a desire to test ourselves. And here we arrive at a critical factor for us as positive thinkers – we need to take risks, but the risks need to be motivating for us rather than a barrier that stops us stretching out into the future.

In the last five years we've seen a huge rise in the popularity of relocation-type TV programmes, where individuals and families move to new countries or overhaul their lives in some way. The popularity of these programmes can be linked to the deep-seated desire in many of us to take risks – or at least an acknowledgement that to get the most from our life we may need to have new experiences. Perhaps some move because deep down they feel unchallenged by what have become very familiar surroundings and feel the need for new 'struggle'. Clearly some undertake the move because they believe the grass will be greener in their new surroundings. Others move because they want something different – not necessarily better, just different.

Watching these programmes provides a real education into the psyche of positive thinkers. Most appear to be prepared. They have a plan of action for when they arrive based on clear GOATs with deadlines for the practical things they will need – children into school, how they will earn money and so on. The test comes when things happen in their new surroundings that they hadn't accounted for. Two things may affect how we deal with problems:

■ Realism

Although we can never factor in all the things that may go wrong in our calculations, an expectation of setbacks along the way can be helpful if we believe we can overcome them – even though we have no way of knowing what those setbacks might be.

This realism is important. Positive thinkers can and should have negative thoughts. Our negative thoughts can give us the balance, which will be critical in setting GOATs that are realistic. Blind optimism is not part of the currency of positive thinking. Negative thoughts needn't hold us back – a realization that life is not all plain sailing makes it more likely that our GOATs will be realistic and therefore met. Whoever it was who said that 'your GOATs minus your doubts equals your reality' was only half right. What you should not be in doubt about is your ability to overcome hurdles. What you should doubt is the notion that reaching your GOATs will be simple.

Being positive means telling ourselves 'there will be setbacks' but that we can overcome them.

■ Motives

If the new journey was undertaken through a desire to 'escape' rather than confront old problems, any setback in the new surroundings will bring us psychologically back to where we were before we started if the old circumstances still exist.

While it is true that putting some space between our difficulties and ourselves can help us to solve old problems, those problems still exist for us. The challenge of the new GOAT should excite us. It shouldn't be an arbitrary point that bears little meaning to our frame of mind.

And ultimately, dealing with challenges comes down to how much we really want to succeed in a new environment. In the case of the relocators, how much did they really want to live the new life they had planned for themselves?

The depth of our problems becomes less important than the recognition that we can deal with them. Some seem to find it a new motivation to look for new solutions. It's a cliché to say that if you wanted to do something and didn't end up doing it or didn't succeed, you didn't want to do it enough. Like most clichés, it has a strong basis in truth.

4 GOAT-scoring

There are three factors that will determine whether we achieve our GOATs or not. They come in a logical sequence:

1 Do I think that I am capable of achieving my GOAT?
2 Do I really want to achieve it?
3 How am I going to set about achieving it?

In Chapter 3 we looked at some of the things that affect factor Number 1 – 'Do I think that I am capable of achieving my GOAT?' Responding to setbacks, building confidence and the desire to develop knowledge and skills are all-important here.

We each have to give an honest answer to factor Number 2 – 'Do I really want to achieve my GOAT?'. Vague wishes (remember the section on being specific at the beginning of this chapter), unless they get translated into specific GOATs, remain as they are. We hear people say, 'I wish I could...' without realizing that in many situations we can make the leap from fantasy to reality if we want to do it enough.

Many readers will have come across the phrase 'Getting in the zone' and this can be a great way of channelling our thinking towards a specific GOAT (we look at this in more detail opposite). Getting in the zone helps us do two things. First it shows us that we can succeed and gives us a sense of what success could feel like. Second, it should create a huge desire in us to go and deliver. Sometimes we can simply ask ourselves, 'Just imagine what it would feel like if...' and we are able to take ourselves to what would be the pinnacle of achievement for us. If we can't excite ourselves with the prospect of achievement in our chosen arena, there is little point in even starting. Getting in the zone is familiar territory for sports people and other performers but it works equally well for us for both large and small future GOATs. Look at how we might visualize success in the activities we've listed below and then add some of your own. But go one step further. Shut your eyes and take yourself to the place you want to go to. Run a mental rehearsal. Get yourself excited at the prospect of success.

'Just imagine...'
Making a presentation
Saying the words you want to say to an audience eagerly listening to you.

Writing a book
The thrill of first seeing the first hardback edition of your first book.

Running a race
Visualize yourself with a competitor 5 metres (16 feet) in front of you, and gradually 'reeling them in' towards you.

Learning a language
A tougher one because you can't rehearse a language you are yet to learn, but we can imagine the thrill of being understood in Chinese or Spanish or French.

Having a baby
Anticipate the wonderful moment, after the pain, of new life.

Over to you – add some of your own GOATs. What might success feel and look like? Just shut your eyes...

Having the self-belief and the desire are crucial, but the third element – our GOAT strategy – is often overlooked. We need to channel our positive thinking into an approach that is going to work best for us. There is no easy answer here, but what is required is a sense of realism. Sometimes we need to recognize the need for patience because we have to make a long-term commitment to achieve the GOAT. In this situation, 'forcing' things can be counter-productive.

In other situations we may decide that moving fast is essential if we are to seize an opportunity that may disappear as quickly as it came. Where speed is required, we can learn something from Chinese military strategists at the turn of the 20th century who used what they called *suzhan sujue* tactic – rapidly fought and rapidly decided. They used a three-stage process for quick action:

1 Assess the situation.
2 Identify the moment of opportunity in the situation.
3 Develop a 'quick action' strategy based on making the most of the situation.

We can respond in a matter of days, or even hours, if speed is needed. Milestones can still help us check the rightness of our direction and the effectiveness of our actions.

Tanya's story

I remember the situation really well. I had left university and had spent a couple of years doing odd jobs and travelling, but I was now aiming for something a little more permanent and maybe a bit more challenging. I think my mum had had enough of me sitting round the house too! One day I was looking through a newspaper and an advert for a job selling advertising space in a national newspaper jumped out at me. Being young, I was taken in by the glamour of working for a national newspaper and my heart started beating a little faster.

I phoned the number in the advert and they put me under pressure right away – I had to do a spelling test! It seems logical really. You need to be able to spell to input ads, and the test was their way of seeing how I responded to a situation I wasn't bargaining for. Anyway, I passed and I was invited in for an interview. To London I went and the next surprise was that it was a group interview. I had to make a quick assessment of how to respond and behave. Some interviewees pretended to be the most outgoing, gregarious people possible; others couldn't really deal with it. In this situation I thought the best person to be was me. I think what clinched me getting the job was that there was an opportunity in the group interview to shine. The interviewer gave us

30 seconds to talk a little about ourselves. Again I had to think quickly, and I guessed that others might talk in fairly bland terms. I remember football and nightclubs coming out a lot.

I can't even remember what I spoke about now, but I remember it was a bit different. There was one other person in the room who also got a job there (there was more than one vacancy) and I remember he talked about something very different too. He's now a very successful comedian. I just thought that in this situation the best thing to do was to make myself be remembered.

Anyway, the next day I got a call offering me the job – they wanted me to start in four days' time. I had lots of reasons not to take it. It was 100 miles away, I had no money (and neither did my mum) and I had nowhere to live. But I knew it was a great opportunity and I had to take it. It's amazing how quickly you can act when you want to. I went to the bank the next morning, got a short-term loan to cover my initial costs, contacted a friend who said I could sleep on his floor while I searched for somewhere to live, packed my bags, got on the train and four days later I started the job. It was the quickest, most spontaneous and at that time the most life-changing thing I'd done. I wonder how many people miss out because they see the hurdles rather than the opportunity? Or because they see the need to respond quickly as a barrier? Sometimes I think it's that need for speed that shows us at our best.

5 Beware GOAT fixation

SMARTER gives us a great framework to work with, but SMARTER does have risks. Keep some fluidity in your life by thinking about these:

■ Don't be blinded by the big GOAT

One-dimensional living can create one-dimensional thinking. Going after the one big life GOAT might mean the little ones get left behind or that other opportunities remain unnoticed. Focusing on the big GOAT for a while is great. Shutting everything else out for the rest of your life could mean loss of perspective. Keep a few balls juggling. Give yourself some future options.

■ Seek imperfection

Trying to be perfect at everything can stop us trying new things. To become good at something probably means that you were less than good first time out. If you can't accept anything less than perfection, you'll never get to first base because you may not even start. Accepting that you're not going to be fantastic the first time you try something means you'll probably try lots of new things. But if you want to improve, what you tell yourself about your initial failure will be critical.

Try to be an imperfectionist! Pursuing perfection can often blank out personal experimentation as we try to perfect ourselves in only one or two areas of life. We may reduce the amount of time available to try new things, more first-time experiences.

6 Check your behaviour

In this chapter we've focused on GOAT-setting helping us to develop new skills (learning Chinese, for example) or activities such as taking up jogging. What's very real for many of us is that we try to set GOATs based around our behaviour. This can be a tough process, so in the Personal resources section we've included an exercise that will help you to set behavioural GOATs for yourself (Exercise 3, page 183). It will take around ten minutes and, as with some of the other longer exercises in this book, it is optional. These behavioural GOATs can help you in two ways:

■ Identifying the behaviours you need to have to achieve the GOATs you've set yourself.
■ Identifying what behavioural shortcomings have restricted us in the past and where we can look to work at our weaknesses.

There are many who say that behaviour is something so intrinsic – 'leopards never change their spots' – that we cannot change. We are not seeking to become someone else here, but over time many of us do learn what types of behaviour will work for us in certain situations. We learn that losing our temper never works (although some of us fail to learn that lesson!) or that the impatience of youth, while providing the driving force for social change, can often leave us frustrated. As we get older, we try to identify the situations where patience is required or where quick decisions are needed.

The most obvious examples of behaviour change come in sport and politics because they are so high profile. It's rare that political revolutionaries remain dedicated for the whole of their life – look at national leaders around the world and ask what many of them were doing 25–30 years ago. Either the revolution happens, or they start trying different methods to secure their GOATs if their policies aren't working. Many sports people, flushed with the arrogance of youth, learn to adapt their behaviour to achieve the results they want. In their teens tennis players such as Martina Navratilova and Roger Federer were known to have strong emotional outbursts and be petulant – behaviour they successfully controlled. Others, such as John McEnroe, saw no need to compromise, and used their displays of raw emotion to psych themselves up even further.

So we come to our personal challenges. If you've done the exercise at the end of the book, you've probably identified behaviour changes that will get you to where you want to be. If you haven't, don't worry because it can be a simple process to identify situations in the past where we've fallen short and to be honest enough with ourselves to identify where the behaviours we utilized were inappropriate. It could be that, through impatience, we jumped at the first solution and didn't sit back and consider other options, or that someone started shouting at us and we rose to the bait, when keeping calm might have served us better. Try to think about situations where different approaches might have worked more positively for you.

7 Bpos (Be positive)

Txt msg 4 u. Bpos.

AAS	Alive and smiling
FRT	For real though
GA	Go ahead
GFI	Go for it
GIGO	Garbage in, garbage out
KISS	Keep it simple, stupid
SLAP	Sounds like a plan
TBD	To be determined
WTG	Way to go

HTH B4N Hope this helps, bye for now

8 Assess yourself

We all continually assess our capabilities, although for some of us at least this is not always a conscious action. Our assessment is based on our level of self-esteem, and in turn our self-esteem is linked to past achievements, successes and failures and to what we thought the causes of these things were. The more we attribute previous achievements to our own efforts, the more we raise our self-esteem and confidence. In turn, the GOATs we set for ourselves will be based on these past successes and failures. Success in the past is likely to lead to us setting more challenging GOATs in the future.

Past failures that we believe are due to personal failings or the continual intervention of 'bad luck' may mean that the GOATs we set ourselves are less than challenging. We covered success and failure in Chapter 3, but we can summarize here by saying that a higher belief in our capabilities, and our ability to influence outcomes by our own input, are likely to lead us to push for the stretch GOAT rather than the GOAT that leaves us merely treading water. Individual experiences make a huge difference to us, but it's our reaction to them that counts. Seeing these experiences as a valuable part of living and 'growing' makes us inclined to want more of them and we set our GOATs accordingly.

9 Think Japanese

'Different individuals...may be more or less attracted to past, present or future orientations,' says culture expert Fons Trompenaars. We can believe that mistakes in the past can guide us through the present and into our future as we learn from those mistakes (notwithstanding that the mistake of the past might be the success of the future). The present can be interminable and intolerable if we are waiting for something that may never come. As Trompenaars puts it:

> *It is as true to say that our expectations of the future determine our present, as to say our present action determines the future; as true to say that our present experience determines our view of the past, as to say the past has made us what we are today.*

Perhaps the ultimate example of people who truly connect the three time zones are the Japanese, who see past, present and future as close to the same thing and understand intuitively the influence of all three on what they do. It's not for nothing that the Japanese write 250-year business plans!

So what's here for the positive thinker? You might be saying 'future' is best, the assumption being that future thinkers are always the most driven. There is, of course, some truth in this, but it's not quite that simple. The referencing of past successes and failures provides as a rich resource for us positive thinkers as the pull of perceived future achievement or happiness. Many define the present – the physical state we all live in – in terms of our perception of the past and future. Positive thinkers are able to utilize all three time zones in differing combinations to help define personal initiative and action.

The lesson from the Japanese is that our GOATs do not need to be based around personal success. In other cultures of the world, GOAIs can be based around the greater good rather than personal achievement. Indeed, someone in this environment may see personal achievement only in terms of the greater good. Too much focus on the self might be seen as disruptive to the greater good. Having one or two more altruistic GOATs benefits the wider community.

We are shaped by our past experiences, our desire for gratification and happiness in the present and our wish for a better future.

Ponder your own life for a moment and think about how your past successes, failures and mistakes are influencing your thinking now; how your immediate desires are shaping your present and how these may or may not be influencing your future. A fun way to do this is to imagine you are presenting a script idea for a film. Hollywood studios like script ideas summarized in 25 words or less. Try to summarize the story of your life ('What I've done so far') in 25 words or less. Do the same for 'What I want now'. Imagine for 'What I want to be' that you are just about to meet your maker and you're summarizing in less than 25 words what you've done!

How do they connect with each other? Well, they may not connect at all. You may be wanting to run a clean slate. Or you may be driven by a past failure that has made you more determined to get it right next time. Or a past success (a qualification, for example) may be positioning your future for you.

Since this is a future-focused activity, it is important to consider the influence of past and present on your future. What factors could help shape the GOATs that you set for yourself? Make a note of them under the heading 'The influence of past and present on my future GOATs'.

10 Don't wait for extra time

As our past gets longer and our future gets shorter, we become inclined to believe that the theatre of potential success has already performed the play of our life, and it can be tempting to define ourselves by past provable glories rather than what there is still left to do. Ask people what they are capable of doing and they may come up with a list of things they have already done rather than including some things they still want to do. And we are not talking about retirement here. Many in their thirties and early forties are already feeling that there's little left to do. At its extreme it can be a strange sensation to read the 'autobiography' of a 25-year-old sport or music star – although they are probably doing it for the money at that stage!

Refer back to the section 'Learning to learn' in Chapter 3 (page 67) and make a note of the future capabilities you were looking to develop as a reminder that if you're young, you've barely started to live, and if you're moving into the third age, there's so much more to give.

Don't let the theatre of success perform the play of your life – there's still so much more to give.

Some say that they have less energy as they get older and are therefore not likely to be doing the things they want to do. To which we can retort that there is nothing less energizing than a belief that you have little energy or curiosity left in you.

If we ask the question 'What are you capable of?', many will reply in terms of what they've done rather than what they could do. The emphasis is all on the past rather than the future. Alastair Campbell, the former 'spin doctor' to British Prime Minister Tony Blair, once remarked: 'The past is for learning, the future is for living.' It's great to take pride in past achievements, but living in them can be counter-productive if you are trying to think positively about your future. Learning is of course a great reason for looking back because it is future-focused. Asking what we can take from past experience to shape future direction can be very helpful to positive thinkers as we define future possibilities for ourselves.

Experience counts for nothing if you haven't learnt anything from it.

Merely responding to proven abilities, a sort of personal 'playing to the crowd', leaves us open to living in the past. Fine for the re-formed 70s' rock group, but perhaps not for the positive thinker looking for new levels of achievement. Make it a priority to nurture the future.

All of us will retain 'baggage' from the past which we carry through life. As Alastair Campbell's quote implies, all kinds of experiences carry learning opportunities. Just as we can be prone to living on past success, we can also be prone to using past failure as an excuse for not trying again or, indeed, for not trying out new things. The proverb 'Once bitten, twice shy' is much used but true for many. The past failure can be used to shape both a more finely tuned 'intuition' and a desire to get it right next time.

> **Some of the best lessons we ever learn are learnt from past mistakes. The error of the past is the wisdom and success of the future.**
>
> Igor Stravinsky

Athlete Paula Radcliffe illustrated the need to move on from past failure after the 2004 Athens Olympics. She was universally expected to win the gold medal, having set a world record a few months earlier and having easily defeated her rivals, but she dropped out of the race near the 32-km (20-mile) mark. Having previously set a world record two minutes ahead of the one before, she had little to prove to anyone but herself. But reminding herself of her capabilities was key for her. She immediately entered the New York Marathon and won it against some of the world's best athletes. She had to move on, and move on she did.

> **You can't change the past, only come to terms with it.**
>
> Paula Radcliffe after 'failing' at the Athens Olympics

Chapter 6
Oxygenation – getting the freshness back!

❑ Me – the creator!

❑ Ten steps to keeping your thinking fresh

❑ The power of laughter

❑ The sensory pentathlon

❑ The athletic pentathlon

Real life can sometimes bring us down. We're feeling tired, thinking one-dimensionally, able to see only half an hour ahead, and we know we need to freshen ourselves up. But where do we begin?

> *It's because there's some devil in us that drives us to and fro on ever-lasting idiocies. There's time for everything except the things worth doing. Think of something you really care about. Then add hour to hour and calculate the fraction of your life that you've actually spent in doing it. And then calculate the amount of time you've spent on things like shaving, riding to and fro on buses, waiting in railway junctions, swapping dirty stories, and reading the newspapers.*
>
> George Orwell, *Coming Up for Air* (Copyright © George Orwell 1939) by permission of Bill Hamilton as the Literary Executor of the Estate of the Late Sonia Brownell Orwell and Secker & Warburg Ltd

Contemporary gripes might be having to sift through dozens of pointless emails every day and hanging on the phone in the vain hope that we might get to speak to a human being at a call centre.

But this chapter is not about gripes. It's about what the positive thinker can do to, in Orwell's words, 'come up for air'. There are many in the world of positive thinking who become obsessed with the subject of 'thinking about thinking' so that the development of knowledge in this area becomes an end in itself rather than a 'leg-up' to a more fulfilled life. Positive thinking expresses itself as an outward-looking attitude to life rather than an inward-looking self-absorption. Oxygenation is about reaching out and accessing the things that create balance for us. In this book we've identified many of the things we can do to create a richer, more fulfilling life for ourselves. We can do these things better if we are able to remove ourselves from the minutiae of life and freshen up our minds and bodies when we need to.

Oxygenation prevents stagnation.

It seems ridiculous that the most developed countries in the world also have the highest number of people who classify themselves as 'depressed'. Of course, clinical depression is quite different from 'down' feelings that come from a kind of restrictive self-absorption. In fact, the latter lead to so much internalized 'baggage' that we lose our sense of perspective, our sense of humour and our *joie de vivre*. In this chapter we look at ten steps to keeping your thinking fresh, as well as advice on stimulating the five senses, the value of exercise and accessing joy and humour in life.

We begin with that wonderful gift that each of us has – the possibility of creating something new from the power of our own imagination.

▓ Me – the creator!

Parking in San Francisco is a nightmare. There are no spots. We decided that the next time we came we'd bring our own spots with us. We decided to invent portable roll-up spots, like those portable holes they use in cartoons. Or maybe a can of spray-on parking spot remover to get rid of other cars...in the end we said a prayer to Rita, the pagan god of parking spots and meters. We shot out beams of parking karma into the hills ahead of us. We were rewarded with fourteen luxurious feet of car space.

Daniel, in Douglas Coupland's *Microserfs* (Reprinted by permission of HarperCollins Ltd © 1996, Douglas Coupland)

The thing about being creative is that we fashion the future out of our capacity to invent. The joy is that we all have the capacity to be inventive, but sometimes we tell ourselves we're not creative, so we behave that way. Or we have a great idea and dismiss it because 'I want to get back to the real world'. Your real world is the result of your creative thinking and that of previous generations. Perhaps sometimes we think we aren't creative because we don't exercise the creative part of us enough. Our 'Ten steps to keeping your thinking fresh' (page 126) will help here. The less you use, the more you lose.

Creative thinking can help us with problem solving too. Here are two problem-solving exercises to try:

Exercise 1: What's the missing value?
Each boxed shape in the diagram overleaf has a value; the value of the square shape is 8. Each figure given is the sum of the values in the respective row, both horizontal and vertical. Can you work out the missing sum on the bottom row?

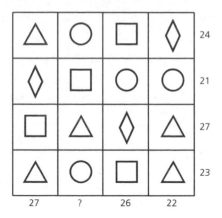

There are two ways to solve this problem. You can approach it by a process of trial and error – trying to work out the value of each of the three other shapes through an elimination process. Or you can go for the solution that requires a bit of a mental leap. By adding up the numbers in the vertical column we get the number 95. The numbers in the horizontal column must add up to 95 as well because you are adding up the sum of the values in both cases. The horizontal column adds up to 75 plus the value of the one we don't know. So now all we need to do is subtract 75 from 95. The answer is 20.

The search for the two correct solutions offer lessons in what we call vertical thinking and lateral thinking. Both terms come from Edward de Bono and were coined in the late 1960s.

■ Vertical thinking – where ideas come from logical, linear thinking processes.
■ Lateral thinking – simply looking at ordinary things in different ways.

Lateral thinking requires leaps of imagination, often using intuition (see Chapter 4) to get from one step to another, which have no basis in logical, linear thinking. A great example recently is the design of the iMac computer. The design broke the mould in thinking that people might actually buy a computer because of what it looks like (the leap of imagination) as well as what it can do (the logical solution). The result at the time of writing is three generations of design innovation and a mindset that helped develop the style and form of the iPod.

An earlier example was in 1937 when Walt Disney gambled a successful business to create a feature-length animated movie – *Snow White and the Seven Dwarfs*. All around him people were saying that it couldn't be done. Who would want to watch a 90-minute animated movie when five minutes was the industry norm? The answer was just about everybody. And that still holds true today!

Both kinds of thinking – lateral and vertical – are as important as each other. There are times when logical, vertical thinking will help us: when the solution required is the 'vanilla' – simple – one. An example might be that a person who knows how to drive a car will find it relatively easy to apply that knowledge to handling a sit-down mower. It doesn't require a creative rethink on how you might go about it. But there are times when the jump has to be made, and we need to consider those times when conventional wisdom will not work for us.

The next exercise really does require some lateral thinking to solve it. A clue: think three-dimensionally!

Exercise 2: Get connected

First, take a sheet of paper and draw pictures of three houses, side-by-side in a horizontal row. Underneath these houses draw three boxes to represent suppliers of three public utilities – water, gas and electricity are the most common three. Using a pen or a pencil, connect each of the houses to each of the utilities. The tough part is that none of the nine lines can cut across each other.

This is an exercise in three-dimensional or lateral thinking. The usual method of drawing lines on a two-dimensional piece of paper does not work because the best-case scenario is that only one line crosses – still short of the objective of no lines crossing. A way to solve it is to use literally three dimensions rather than the two dimensions of writing on a flat piece of paper.

So a couple of solutions are:

■ For the final line lift up the piece of paper, put the pen through the underside of the utility that needs to be connected and bore a hole through it. Then bore a hole through the house it needs to be connected to. Then connect the two holes with the pen or the pencil. Hey presto, the final connection!

■ Another solution is to draw the three houses in horizontal formation with the utilities and draw in the eight lines that you can without crossing over. Then simply fold the paper so that the house and the corresponding utility are next to each other and then put in a very short line.

If you want to exercise the brain, you'll find lots of websites with ideas and activities for doing this. Evidence shows that the brain needs exercising in the way the body does. Mental exercise creates a healthier, more agile mind. In a feature on BBC Radio London a few years ago it was reported that after the brains of London taxi drivers were studied over an extended period of time it appeared that the part of the brain responsible for spatial awareness (which they used to navigate around London) had grown significantly. So perhaps our brain is like our muscles – the more we use it, the stronger it gets.

Oxygenating the mind to help us solve problems and generate solutions with open-minded thought processes is essential for us as positive thinkers. What we are encouraging here is for the positive thinker to be a proactive thinker. And there are many ways in which the mind can be proactive.

Ten steps to keeping your thinking fresh
1 The mental dimmer switch

You can't idle your way to insight. On the other hand, 'forcing' your mind to come up with a continual supply of new solutions can be counter-productive. The mind can be at its least playful, its least imaginative and its least receptive when it's forced into a corner.

Think of the cat apparently fast asleep in front of a warm log fire. A mouse runs past. In a flash the cat has the mouse in its paws. The cat combines the apparently contradictory notions of engagement with the world and temporary withdrawal from it.

Sometimes consciously disengaging from a difficult problem for a time can declutter the mind and help it return to a more relaxed state. Controlling the 'mental dimmer switch' doesn't mean you switch the lights out altogether. Sometimes positive thinkers need to try not to think. And in the process of 'not thinking' may come the breakthrough.

The mental dimmer switch gives us the time we need for the brain to tussle with possible solutions without our fully conscious state throwing in the extra wattage that may hinder rather than help our thinking.

A positive thinker shouldn't feel the need to be vigorously wrestling with challenges, problems and conundrums all the time. In mental processes that are only barely understood, our brain continues to work even when we are not conscious of it doing so. The 'eureka' moment may not come about entirely by accident.

Here are some tips.

- Consciously try to stop thinking. Switch off from the challenge or problem.
- At what times can you blank out challenges and problems? In the bath? Riding a bicycle? Cooking a meal?
- Write down those 3 a.m. 'eureka' thoughts. Pen and paper by the bed?

A dimmer switch in the shower

Steve liked showering. He liked showering because he got all his best ideas in the shower cubicle. He would shut off his mind and enjoy the water and suddenly he'd find solutions coming to him. He realized, however, that when he got out of the shower and back to his normal state the thoughts were disappearing. He decided to install a board with a water-resistant pen in the shower so he could jot down his ideas before returning to the serious business of showering.

How do you remember things? Where could you use your own dimmer switch?

Lesson: Forcing yourself to think can be counter-productive. Slowing down the mind can lead to a solution that 'hard-search' thinking often fails to find.

2 Change routine

A hundred years ago there was an obscure group at Oxford University called the Histeron-Proteron Society, whose members lived the day in reverse. They would get up and immediately drink brandy and port, then eat cheese, have their pudding followed by main course, fish course, a starter and then an aperitif. Perhaps a bit of time at the club afterwards. And of course all of this would be done in formal evening wear. The day would finish with the newspapers and a breakfast of kedgeree or kippers. The upper classes being as they were in those days, they probably didn't fit in a whole lot of time for working, whatever kind of day they were living!

Any readers wanting to try it are of course welcome, but the lesson here is about breaking the routine of conventional thinking and day-to-day living.

What could you do to add a little freshness to your usual day-to-day existence? What could you do differently?

Lesson: Persistent routine creates stagnant thoughts. Changing routine turns the mind into a fast-flowing river of ideas.

3 What's the problem?

'I'm not returning until you fix it,' bandleader Count Basie told a club owner whose piano was always out of tune. A month later Basie got a call that everything was fine. When he returned, the piano was still out of tune. 'You said you fixed it!' an irate Basie exclaimed. 'I did,' came the reply. 'I had it painted.'

Roger von Oech, *A Whack on the Side of the Head*

Lesson: When solving problems, try to make sure you are solving the right problem.

4 How might somebody else see it?

'Why does my owner always feed me when I rub up against her?' asked the cat. 'Why does my cat rub up against me when it wants feeding?' asked the owner.

Try to see the world from the perspective of others. What seems obvious to you might be viewed very differently by others.

So, try to ask yourself the following questions if you want a more rounded, balanced view:

- Why do I see things this way?
- How might others see it?
- Why might they be seeing things their way?
- What's important to them?
- Is my perspective too narrow and self-centred?

Lesson: Travel to the 6 billion worlds of your fellow human beings.

5 What assumptions?

How many of us have spent time crouched over a piece of malfunctioning electrical equipment, wondering why it doesn't work, until we realized it wasn't plugged in?

or

When we tried to solve the 'get connected' problem earlier in this chapter, did we assume that you have to work in two dimensions to solve it?

or

Did we assume that the fastest British person in the 2003 London Marathon would be a man? (It was Paula Radcliffe.)

Lesson 1: Making assumptions about 'the way things are' reduces the possibilities for 'the way things could be'.

Lesson 2: Making assumptions about our own capabilities means we only live up to the level of the assumption.

In tough times it's easy to limit your thinking by inaccurately defining your problems and therefore restricting the range of options open to you. Crisis of situation often breeds crisis of thinking. How many of us, when we reflect on problems that we've had in the past, are able to see the problem as it really was? It's much easier to apply an appropriate solution retrospectively when the judgement is not impaired by anxiety. What we find is that we have often made a whole batch of assumptions about what we can or cannot do to resolve the situation.

Information-gathering is key. If we think we know it all, we shut off the possibilities of other solutions and stop information-gathering.

Lesson 3: Challenge the way you see something now by imagining yourself in the future 'looking back'.

6 Psychological rioting

Living in the 'comfort zone' is a risky business. Things often change at the point when we're least prepared to meet those changes. The key is to set the future agenda. Indulge in some 'psychological rioting' to create multiple possible futures for yourself.

Ask these 'What' questions to help your personal 'riot':

What if?
What if I tried this? Where might it take me?

What's new?
Keep up to date with new ideas. What could I have missed? What's next?

What could happen?
This is a positive and a negative statement. In weighing up the pros and cons of something, ask 'What could happen?' as a question based in future possibilities as well as 'What could happen?' as a question based in future loss.

What don't I know?
Is there a gap in my knowledge that means I may struggle in the future?

What fun?
Am I enjoying myself as much as I could be? Am I accessing enough of the things that give me pleasure?

What am I assuming?
Am I creating my own reality by assuming that my present is my future? What can I change (which I may be presuming that I can't)?

Who?
We are automatically attracted to people who have similar views, opinions and tastes to ourselves. Try spending time with people who think differently. Give yourself different perspectives.

People who have an entrenched, unseeing view of the world become a parody of themselves. And we end up conforming to the stereotype that characterizes the like-minded people we try to surround ourselves with.

Lesson 1: It's OK to create some confusion in your thinking. As business guru Tom Peters said, 'Anyone who isn't confused, isn't thinking clearly.'
Lesson 2: Use a riot in your thinking to create a revolution in your life.

7 That's impossible?

We can and will create things for ever. Imagine what people would have said 100 years ago if we'd told them that post 2000 people would have:

- enjoyed relative peace in western Europe for 60 years
- landed a probe on Titan
- created a system that sends messages around the world in a few seconds
- seen a 65-year-old woman give birth.

What things do you imagine we might create in the next 50–100 years? A personal microchip in the head that acts as TV/computer/mobile phone/ games console (and sends email around the world by thought)? A man giving birth? The first conversation with extraterrestrials? Peace in the Middle East? Someone somewhere is probably working on these things right now. Will developments that currently seem frightening (microchips in our head, for example) be seen as normal in 100 years' time?

All it often takes for humans to begin the process of invention is to have the idea in the first place and be brave enough to put the idea into practice in the face of lots of people saying it can't be done.

Let's think about our own life and that 'can't be done' mentality. If we tell ourselves that something 'can't be done', we won't do it, thereby instantly creating the reality we assumed in the first place. The lesson here for us is that in the process of oxygenating our life – breathing new energy into the present and the future – we often limit future possibilities by assuming a 'can't be done' mentality. Have a think about your own life for moment.

Twenty years ago what did you imagine you would be doing now? (You don't have to answer this one if you're 20 now!)

What do you think you'll be doing in 20 years' time?

What would you *like* to be doing in 20 years' time?

OK, what's stopping you? Well, I admit if you are 60 years old you might not win next year's Chicago Marathon. But in 100 years' time a 60-year-old might. Or a woman might win the men's 100-metre Olympic final.

Lesson: Today's fantasy is tomorrow's norm. What could be fantastic about your future?

8 Joining unrelated concepts: what if?

This extends the 'psychological riot' we looked at in Number 6 (page 129). Think of something you are pondering about doing that you haven't quite got round to yet. Write down the reasons that you haven't quite got round to it. Now write down the 'What if?' responses. Ask yourself (with a positive slant) what the possibilities are of undertaking a particular action. If you find yourself being motivated by those possibilities – your heart perhaps beating a little faster – ask a further question. 'Why not?'

Lesson: Asking 'What if?' builds the bridge between today's ideas and tomorrow's reality.

9 Accentuate the positive

It's been said that the reason peace negotiations break down is that the two warring factions instantly get mired in the things they disagree about. Why not start the peace talks discussing the things they agree about? It sets the right tone when they get on to the things they really need to resolve.

In the same way, why get bogged down with the faults in an idea or a solution? Can you take what's good about something and leave the bad bit behind?

Lesson: Breathe life into ideas and solutions by accentuating the good bits. Don't kill them off by concentrating on the bad.

10 Build a mental hinterland

Viktor Frankl, in his book about life in a concentration camp (*Man's Search for Meaning*), observed the capacity to survive among those who were forced into hard labour. He acknowledged that many of those who arrived at the camp were dead within 12 hours or so. However, having been put to work, he decided to set himself the task of observing those around him – what made some of them survive? It seemed obvious that those with the physical attributes of size, musculature and experience of hard physical labour would be the most likely to get through. The reality was different. He found, in the toughest of circumstances, that those who had a psychological resource to 'escape' to were more likely to make it. These could be people who had a rich intellectual life before the war and who wanted to continue their work. Or it might have been cherished memories of loved ones they hoped to see when they got out. As Frankl says, 'They were able to retreat from their terrible surroundings to a life of inner riches and spiritual freedom.'

I hope that no reader of this will have to resort to such an extreme 'mental hinterland' in order to overcome external catastrophe, but its lesson is simple for us in much less difficult circumstances. A personal life with meaning acts as a resource for us to live in when circumstances are tough. This doesn't mean we stick our head in the sand. It merely means that enrichment gives us balance – a true sense of perspective. This perspective allows us to be more rational about the things that are causing us difficulty.

Think about where your own mental hinterland lies. It doesn't have to be related to career. It could be a consuming hobby or it could be your children or grandchildren. Can you write a sentence that describes the things that really add meaning to your own life?

If you're struggling to write this, don't worry – but do begin to think positively about accessing some of the things, in George Orwell's words, 'that you really care about'. Use the chart below to help you think about developing your own hinterland. I've filled in the columns with examples, but yours might include things like relationships with family or friendships that you've neglected. And putting a deadline on such actions will make it more likely that you turn the thought into reality.

Things to try	Action	By when
Wine-tasting	Enrol in classes at local college	31 August – for the new term
Find out more about psychology	Buy a good introductory book	End of next week
Find things that cost nothing to do	Web search	By Friday

It is perfectly OK to have things on this list that seem to have no obvious learning benefit – other than the learning for learning's sake. Don't always believe earnest educationists who insist on learning outcomes. Sometimes do it just for fun and maybe to 'tickle' a part of the brain that doesn't usually get 'tickled'. Who knows where the 'tickle' will take you? We build lots of confidence and self-esteem when we learn new things.

I knew a very successful advertising executive who, even with little free time, made sure that once a week she indulged in a hobby completely unrelated to her work – and she changed the hobby every year. At the time I knew her it was pottery. When I questioned her she said that she had to have something else in her life so that she stopped work taking over. She said that she loved her job but that she didn't want it to be the only thing in her life. She now heads up a very successful small ads paper.

Lesson: Develop something in your life that gives you somewhere to go to mentally when you need time out from the routine or from tough times.

■ The power of laughter

Sometimes, in our darkest moments, someone is able to say something that breaks the tension or the negative feelings that are building inside us. In other situations it can be interesting to observe people who really do have problems and challenges ahead of them but who haven't lost their ability to find things to enjoy and laugh at. In this section we look at some of the skills we can develop to help maintain balance and perspective when we really need to.

But even if you haven't got problems, there's nothing like a bit of fun to remind us that life is for enjoying. Sometimes we just need to remind ourselves to keep up a humorous perspective.

Dying of dead seriousness

Writer and self-styled 'humaerobacist' – specializing in humour skills – C.W. Metcalf tells a lovely story about how he realized he was, in his words, 'dying of dead seriousness'. As a highly stressed and 'sick' (to him) photo-journalist, he was given an assignment in the children's ward of a cancer hospital where all the patients were terminally ill. When he walked into the ward the first thing that struck him was the amount of laughter and joy there was. While he observed the environment, a terminally ill child pulled at his trouser leg from the bed he was lying in and said quite simply, 'Do you want to sit down? You don't look too good.'

C.W. is bald and maybe the child thought he was a cancer patient too. In that moment, when C.W. thought he must look really ill to the child, he realized that some things had to change. The young boy, despite his circumstances, was able to think of others, while C.W.'s life had lost all sense of perspective as he'd become wrapped up and consumed by his own little world. He hadn't drawn breath properly for years and learnt to enjoy what was around him – everything was 'serious'. Often we don't really see what's around us until there's a chance that it might not be there any more.

As a 'humaerobacist', C.W. says that his business is not in analysing humour. He rightly points out that this is like dissecting a frog: you know all about the frog but – no frog! His business is in helping us laugh – in taking life and ourselves a little less seriously.

There's a chance – but only a chance – that your changed approach can be born out of a 'eureka' experience like the one C.W. had. For C.W. it may have been a refined sense of his own mortality; perhaps he realized he was subconsciously taking himself closer to his maker because of his highly stressed condition. Things had to change and they did. C.W. was able to flick a switch. For some readers the change will happen over a longer period of time – but you do need to be receptive to the idea of change, if change is what you need.

Dead seriousness is not a healthy condition. Many of us can recall particular types of manager who walked around the office red-faced and grouchy, taking themselves far too seriously. Their mindset made them ill-equipped to do anything about the problem themselves.

So where do we start?

Perhaps our best recourse is to laugh at ourselves. Remember that time when you did something accidentally funny but were a little embarrassed and hid. A good friend once told me of a time when she walked the length of Kensington High Street in London with her dress tucked into her underwear at the back – no one told her until she'd been walking for a good ten minutes. She laughs for ages when she recounts that story now.

Our recourse here is for us to be able to laugh at ourselves while recognizing that we are not positioned at the Earth's core with the rest of the world revolving around us. Learning to laugh at our circumstances and ourselves helps us to keep a balanced view of our personal world. Are you able to identify your own humour blind spot? Can you find humour/enjoyment in some aspect of your life that may be causing you personal difficulty?

A balanced mindset helps the positive thinker put the problem into perspective and thus in a better position to solve it, or at least come to terms with it, successfully.

Laugh lines

Laughter lives best in spontaneity, and its catalyst comes from our interactions with others. If we don't make the effort to laugh – through enriching our social laugh-life, making friends or building personal relationships, for example – we shut off a rewarding path to life's most natural painkiller.

Think about the last time you let rip with your best laugh – when you completely forgot everything and did the most natural thing in the world. It was a wonderful experience for me a few years ago, when visiting a very poor country and looking out of the hotel window, to see a group of impoverished children totally immersed in playing with an old bike tyre for what seemed like hours. The smiles never left their faces. Why are some people able to access fun and laughter when they have ten times the problems that we have? Why do some of the most deprived countries in the world produce some of the most joyous music?

Just think for a moment of some of the benefits of laughing more:

- It lowers blood pressure.
- It releases endorphins (natural painkillers).
- It helps to make sure life is enjoyed not endured.
- It makes sure the bad bits in life don't win.
- It helps keep a sense of perspective.
- It often comes from a shared memorable experience – how many 'Remember the time when…' conversations do we have?

Although laughing comes best from spontaneity, why not keep one of your favourite comedy videos to hand – a *Friends* or a *Frasier*, a *Fawlty Towers* or *The Office* – and pop it in the DVD player when you really need to laugh. Or make a conscious decision to regularly access whatever it is that makes you laugh. Laughter comes more easily to those who want to laugh. The best times are often the most spontaneous and, as someone I know once said, 'You can't teach spontaneous'. And that person was right. But you can choose to act on some of the whims we have all the time rather than just ignoring them. And you'll have fun while you're doing it.

■ The sensory pentathlon

Our five senses – taste, touch, smell, sight and hearing – need a workout as much as our bodies do. If we don't keep them in shape, there's the danger of 'none-sense' – when the pressures of everyday living make us desensitized. In the state of 'none-sense' we can find ourselves continually responding to everybody else's pace without slowing down to stimulate and reinvigorate our own senses. Or we may find ourselves barely responding to things that happen around us. The zombified state of many of those dragging themselves to work on the New York Subway or the London Tube clearly shows our ability to exist while being barely conscious of what's going on around us. We lose our ability to truly 'sense'.

Glen's story

Glen was having some trouble. He wasn't really happy, but couldn't quite fathom why. Things were going OK for him. He had a reasonable job, a new girlfriend and he was looking after himself too. One weekend he went to stay with a friend in the country. His friend's house was 8 km (5 miles) from the nearest town. Perfect, he thought, for a short break – and so it proved.

My friend, who knew I wasn't very happy, had thought about what to do for the weekend. He had spent a fortune on about 20 kinds of fruit, far more than we could ever eat. We made a giant fruit salad, *Guinness Book of Records* territory, and had real fun with the simplest experience imaginable, chopping up the fruit, seeing how small we could get each piece – a bit like when you keep folding a piece of paper to see how small you can get it. And the eating of it was great. All the different flavours. I remember thinking silly things, such as I wonder what it will be like if I mix a piece of banana with a bit of papaya and so on, and we tried to explain the mix of flavours to each other. We must have been doing this for about four hours. Not that either of us had any notion of looking at a clock. We just completely got lost in what we were doing. I remember the pair of us sitting in his lounge and laughing at the amount of gurgling and fermentation going on in our stomachs!

The next day I left my friend and cycled the five miles to the station. I find it quite difficult to express what happened next because it was so personal but I remember that it was springtime and the trees were in blossom and the sky was perfectly blue and the sun was exploding out of the sky and for about ten seconds, I'm not really sure, I felt absolutely fantastic. I'd laughed at people who had described being at one with nature, but I suppose that's exactly how I felt. It's funny because I don't really like the countryside; I'm a city person. But it was exactly what I needed. I just stopped and tried to capture the moment. I knew I had to.

I think I needed to remind myself of what was important. Sometimes it just happens like that. When I analyse that weekend I think of two parts: the first being a fun experience shared with a true friend, the second being something that was totally mine. What my friend and I did was silly to everyone else in the world, but it became special to me. I carried that weekend with me for the next ten years of my life and I still recall it when I need to. It was beautiful. I snapped out of whatever it was I was feeling and learnt to enjoy the things I was doing more. And I still don't really know why it should have been like that. Every part of me was fulfilled by simplicity. That's all I can say.

So the challenge for us as positive thinkers becomes one of reinvigorating the five senses. Here are some possibilities:

Taste

If you've seen the wonderful film of Henry Fielding's classic novel *Tom Jones*, you will recall the moment when Tom and a pretty young woman turn dinner into an erotic feast with mouthfuls of food savoured and swallowed as though they were an integral part of the love-making that would inevitably follow. Wouldn't it be great if food meant that much to us more often?

I recall one moment in my life when my dinner guest was in a hurry because he was off to dinner with someone else after me. Under those circumstances how can anyone enjoy something that gets to the very core of human survival – feeding ourselves?

The success of celebrity chefs, such as Martha Stewart in the USA (before her imprisonment for insider trading) or Jamie Oliver in the UK, bears testimony to our desire to take pleasure in food. But the watching of food programmes on television has become a spectator sport rather than Inspiring us to go off and cook for ourselves. We've got the cookbook, but how often do we use it?

For many of us in the UK or USA, dinner begins when we've got the kids to bed. It's interesting that in countries that really appreciate their food, France and Italy, for example, eating is a communal experience with some-times more than one family eating together. They manage to slow down and enjoy the most natural of pursuits with those who are important to them. The process of eating is energizing rather than soporific.

Thirty years ago Americans had the highest life expectancy in the world. At the time of writing the USA is 46th on the list (*CIA Factbook*, 2005). There may be many reasons for this, but it's hard to believe that a culture that sees the eating of food as something akin to the way that stokers used to throw coal into the fire of a steam train is not part of the equation. And the rest of the world is not far behind.

The lesson here is a simple one. Good food (and good company while we eat that food) is good for us. We have to eat. Why not draw breath and take your time over it?

Touch
When did you last sift some soil through your hands? Or run your fingers through your children's hair? Or make a loaf of bread? Or stroke a content-edly purring cat? Or wear silk close to your skin?

Smell
With the majority of Western world inhabitants choosing to live in urban environments, the word 'smell' will be only too familiar to them. Even in agrarian economies, mass migration to the cities has accelerated. With the acridity of the air in many of these places – and the proliferation of eye-watering fake smells, such as car fresheners – it's not surprising that we are inclined to shut off this most potent of senses. It's the one most directly linked to the brain, triggering immediate responses.

Wonderful smells cleanse us and evoke images that take us to happy places – many of them connected to childhood: our classroom, Sunday lunch, the seaside, a walk in the park. We remind ourselves that they exist even if we're not there at that moment and can only imagine the smell. Great natural smells are emotional purifiers.

Carla's story

My partner was busy working on his computer when I walked into his office and the smell of a fresh apple hit me. He'd just eaten one of those hard green apples, Granny Smith's I think they are. It took me straight back to my school days. Every day my mum would pop an apple into my satchel for me to eat during my morning break at school. I remember that while I was eating my apple, all my friends were tucking into cakes and sweets.

I've smelt that smell many times since, but at that moment it just took me back to my childhood immediately and of course I wanted to go back and have a look at my old school. My five-year-old daughter had been questioning me about my schooldays – she's just started school herself. And I thought, why don't we both go? I can show her round and give her an idea about what school was like for me. So a few days later we went. I've never known my daughter so quiet! She hung on every word I was saying about the things I did there when normally I can't get a word in edgeways. I could just tell she was absolutely fascinated. We played on the grass outside for a bit, had a walk around the woods at the bottom of the playground, and even though it was holiday time, we were able to look around the classrooms.

Of course, the thing I remembered straight away wasn't the building or the furniture but the smell! After about an hour there we went off into the town and had a drink and then the questions started coming out. Sometimes children's continual questions can be demanding, but that day I loved answering them. We talked like two friends for ages. It was a lovely day for me. All from the smell of an apple!

See

It's often said that, to get a real view of London, you need to look up. Or, to get the view of 'London under London', look down. It could easily be said about San Francisco, Johannesburg or Sydney too. But of course most of us look straight ahead at the things we've always looked at wherever we are. The same row of shops, the train station, the bus stop, the semi-familiar faces all exist as part of a narrow panorama that provides us with familiarity.

It's a stimulating exercise to view your local area as a tourist might. Take a view of your environment that isn't your natural one. Ask what's down that narrow street you've never walked along before, or what's in that little museum you've never visited but were always curious about. And if you find yourself in a big city, such as London, look up and enjoy the architecture, or be amazed at how many mini-worlds exist in the cramped but remarkable environment that is Hong Kong. If you're in the countryside, why not revert to schooldays and spread a white sheet under a tree, bash the branches and observe the mass of life that drops out of it?

In the south of France is a man named Patrick, whose wife died three years ago. He's lived in the region all his life, but since his wife died he's made a conscious effort to visit a new place in his area at least once a week. He takes these journeys to keep himself stimulated. He says he never realized how much there was to see until he made a conscious effort to go and see it. And he doesn't envisage running out of places to explore in the near future.

Hear

There was once a young man called John, who for about a month was troubled at night by a very quiet but high-pitched whistle that seemed to come from somewhere in his bedroom. He reckoned that it must relate to some sort of electrical gadgetry, but nothing seemed to be switched on. During the day he couldn't really hear it because of all the extraneous noise associated with the daytime. Eventually he worked out that it was coming from the computer. Even though the computer was switched off, it was still plugged in and clearly not quite asleep itself.

Being a curious man, John wondered what might happen if he tried to remove all incidental noise in the house. How much persistent noise pollution was there gnawing away at his subconscious? The hum of the fridge, the drip of a tap, the fly buzzing at the window, the creak and gurgle of the central heating. He made sure the radio was off and the phone unplugged too. And then he sat down and listened again. What was remarkable, he says, was that, although he was vaguely conscious of the noise outside his house, whirring away to itself, he felt part of another world, an indoor world where he was able to enjoy…nothing…apart from the sound of silence.

Below is a simple chart to help us think about stimulating our own senses. Copy it on to a sheet of paper, and in 'The last time' column write in the last time you can remember each of those senses being stimulated in a pleasurable, memorable way. There are some suggestions for 'The next time' column – but why not fill in some of your own? This isn't to suggest a 'planned' life, as the following section makes clear, but sometimes we need to make a conscious effort to access the things that give us joy.

My sensory pentathlon

Sense	The last time	The next time
Taste	_____	Cooking a great meal?
Touch	_____	Out in the garden?
Smell	_____	A new brand of coffee?
See	_____	The night sky?
Hear	_____	A new piece of music?

Spontaneity

It may sound a contradiction in terms, but we can try to be more spontaneous when accessing the stimulation of our five senses. In 'The last time' column circle those times that were spontaneous. How many out of five? We have spontaneous ideas all the time – sometimes just switching from a 'wouldn't it be great if' to 'why not do it now' mentality is all that is required. Spontaneous things can often be the most rewarding because we were not expecting them. Remember the meticulously planned event that didn't quite do it for you when the 'let's go out and have a good time now' evening ended up being really memorable?

■ The athletic pentathlon

The Ancient Greeks invented the pentathlon – five athletic events that were designed to equip warriors with a range of skills essential in battle. We can thus begin to understand where our modern version, consisting of horse riding, fencing, swimming, running and pistol shooting, has come from.

Fortunately, we don't need battle skills any more, but we still need to be sure we have the physical resilience required to survive and thrive on the pressures of modern-day living. In fact, our bodies have evolved through history to need regular exercise. What's your own 'modern' pentathlon? Can you think of five physical activities you could attempt to get your physical wellbeing up to scratch? Try out a few different things and see what's right for you. We are all different and some kinds of exercise will be right for us and some less so. Some of us need the rigour of hard, competitive sport, while others may respond better to activities such as yoga.

The positive effects of exercise are well known, including the following.

■ We release beta-endorphins, which create a feeling of well-being in us.
■ Exercise removes feelings of tension and stress – tight muscles and sinews become loose.
■ Exercise takes you psychologically away from your problems for a time, and can help you come back to them refreshed.
■ Exercise helps to clear the mind of emotional baggage, making problem-solving easier. Many of us have experienced the 'eureka' moment (see 'The mental dimmer switch' on page 126) when undertaking exercise.
■ Fit, healthy bodies are less susceptible to debilitating illnesses.

What's less well publicized is that physical exercise helps the mind to think positively. Who feels worse after exercise than they did before? If we haven't exercised in a long time, we may feel a bit 'trashed' immediately afterwards, but that feeling soon turns into a warming glow – some even describe it as a natural 'high'. And we add to that healthy physical feeling with the self-pride we experience by getting away from the electronic goldfish bowl (television) and doing something positive.

The positive thinker values the clean, fresh thinking that physical exercise can bring. The hardest bit is to jump the first hurdle and positively decide to go and do it.

A final thought...
Whether it's something from the physical or sensory pentathlon, try to do something each day just for yourself.

Not many of us on our death-bed will say, 'I wish I'd spent more time at the office'. But we might say, 'I wish I'd had more fun while I was there!'

Chapter 7
Playing for a living

❏ Why do I go to work?

❏ Choosing to 'play' at work

❏ Getting in the 'flow'

❏ Living through change

❏ It's all in the timing

❏ Breaking habits

❏ Nobody's choice but mine

❏ Working positively

■ Why do I go to work?

So do you go to work or do you go to play? Ever since industrializing economies became more complex in the 19th century, we've felt the need to add structure to the day – we created a more rigid framework to live by in order for us to make sense of our world. Our 'work' structured our 'time' because 'time' became more important. But as our minds have switched from a production mentality to a 'What am I getting out of this?' mentality, we have started to ask ourselves more and more questions about the nature of our work.

Recognizing that we are likely to spend 80,000–100,000 hours of our life at 'work', we are, quite justifiably, asking for more than a living.In previous ages we were paid just enough to provide for food and shelter, but the industrial economies realized they needed markets (the self-same 'workers') to buy their products and had to pay more so that we could buy more. This is perhaps a response to the extreme comfort most of us are able to experience in the post-industrial age. We've satisfied the need for food, shelter and much else besides (the original reasons for us to go 'to work') – what else is there for us? In the consumer age we've learnt to search for wants rather than needs because many of us earn far more than we need to satisfy the basic requirements for living.

What gets me to work?

To help you think about why you go to work, try doing the next exercise. It helps us to think about what's important to us at our work. Try to spend some time really thinking about this. The responses that jump into your head instantly may not be the responses you give when you think about it a little. Look at the list below and rank the entries in order of importance to you personally: from 1 as the most important to 15 as the least important. Try not to rank any as equals because the exercise is as much concerned with thinking about what is important to you and to rank accordingly. If you are starting with the number 1 ranking and finding it difficult, why not start at the least important? Work backwards.

Do the exercise first and then read on.

I go to work because…

It gives me a sense of achievement ☐

I need regular challenges ☐

It enables me to express myself ☐

It helps develop my knowledge and skills ☐

My job is interesting ☐

I can meet new people there ☐

My work colleagues are my friends ☐

I enjoy doing things for others ☐

My work gives me a social life ☐

It gets me out of the house ☐

I like the responsibility ☐

I need my salary ☐

It gives me security ☐

I like the status that my work gives me ☐

I can have some fun there ☐

Elements of this list have been inspired by the work of Frederick Herzberg.

So which ones were you struggling to prioritize? Did your own findings surprise you? Where did salary sit in the ranking? Is it all-important to you?

The big question that many of us ask is where to put salary. Most assume that we go to work for money, but there is an old saying that 'We go to work for money when it is the only thing to go to work for'! I've used this exercise with many people to help them understand the things that are important to them, and most are surprised how low down the scale money comes. Readers who are managers may want to try this with those they manage as a way of understanding them better.

This is not to diminish those readers who placed salary at, or near, the top of their personal league table. In many professions, such as selling, the desire for money needs to be a prime motivating factor. Perhaps what is important is that readers who have identified salary as crucial to them are in a profession where that aspiration can be fulfilled. If salary is number 1 for you, there is little point in being a charity worker, for example. Readers from countries where jobs are at a real premium may place salary nearer the top of the scale.

Understanding why we go to work helps us do a number of things:

■ It helps us feel more positively about our work because we recognize why it is so important to us.
■ It can help us seek work that gives us what we want from our work.
■ If we are unhappy in our work it can pinpoint the reasons why.
■ Once we are fully conscious of the things that are most important to us, we are more inclined to actively seek those things.

■ Choosing to 'play' at work

We may not be entirely conscious of it, but many of us would secretly admit the lunacy of wanting more and more, working harder and harder to pay for it, then wanting still more because we are not altogether happy with our relentless work (and therefore need comfort), then buying more and so on. In those circumstances, it's no wonder that work can be a real grind. We become slaves to the job.

The answer may come in the way we see our work. We can try to understand:

■ How important it is for us to have an 'occupation' – whatever that may be.
■ If we take that occupation too seriously, we will enjoy it less and be much less effective while we are doing it.
■ We can enjoy our work if we want to *and* get to a point beyond enjoyment – fulfilment – where our occupation gives us many of the things we want from life.

Notice that we have switched from the word 'work' to the word 'occupation'. Our occupation is the thing that fills the bulk of our day. For most of us that happens to be what we would traditionally call our work. We need to be occupied. It just so happens that in Western societies that means the office, the factory, the shop, the building site, the warehouse or the car.

Let us accept that we have to be there. If we have to be there, we then have a simple further choice.

■ Am I going to do the best I can to enjoy myself or not?

There is only one answer for us as positive thinkers. We then need to answer a follow-up question:

■ Am I going to do the best I can to enjoy myself because I have to or because I want to?

Finding enjoyment in work happens only if we really *want* to enjoy it.

And so we arrive through our 'desire', our 'want', at the point where we seek to enjoy ourselves. We are now in a much better position to 'play'. We're doing it because we want to.

■ Learning to 'play' at work

The word 'play' makes us think of leisure activities or children. It is not a word usually associated with work, yet it is crucial in helping us get to the end of the day with some sense of enjoyment. As Pat Kane, formerly of pop band Hue and Cry and now an author and critic, says in *The Play Ethic*, 'The opposite of play is depression.' Aristotle saw play purely as 'non-laborious activity'.

But many see the opposite of play as work. What we are saying here is that we can apply the thinking we traditionally utilize in one situation – when we play – and apply that thinking to another – when we work. They are not mutually exclusive. We've come a long way from a dictionary definition that says that 'to play' means 'to take part in enjoyable activity for the sake of amusement'. Play has become a watchword for something much deeper than that. It's really about expressing the best side of us as human beings.

Make a note of some of the feelings you have when you engage in leisure activities and hobbies. Look at the list. Do they sound like the feelings we want to have at work too?

When we are engaging in leisure activities we feel much more able to 'express' ourselves because it's such a proactive word. If we want to express ourselves and play at work, we need to be a 'player' not a 'spectator'. We cannot rely on anyone else to create the enjoyable workplace for us – least of all our employer. We have to find it within ourselves. There are many things we can do to 'play'. Overleaf are some suggestions to get you started:

■ Get in there!

We won't start to play if we wait for other people to tell us when we can. We play best when we choose to engage and truly connect with our work. Play is about freedom of expression. Play is about doing what comes naturally to us. Play is about keeping interested, curious, experimental, creative, positive, affirming, encouraging, sharing. We all have at least some of those things in us. We 'play' best when we have found them. Be proactive and be yourself.

What we tell ourselves about our work will come out in our behaviour. We create our own reality at work through the language we use.

My thinking	My reality
Interesting	I'm stimulated
Boring	I'm bored
Challenging	I'm fulfilled
Fun	I have fun!

What are you telling yourself about the work you do? Keep your language and your thinking positive. Work can be enjoyed rather than endured.

■ Remind yourself why you come to work

Just make a note now of the top three or four reasons you come to work in the first place (see 'What gets me to work?', page 146). Which of those are all the more enjoyable for a little playfulness?

And remember: over 50 per cent of us meet our life partner at work, so we must have been enjoying ourselves somewhere down the line!

■ Consider the possibilities of being 'playful'

Children play all the time. What do we know about children? They are open-minded, they are receptive to ideas, they see no barriers to creativity, they learn quickly, they can occupy themselves with almost anything, they show their emotions, they haven't learnt to be callous, cold, manipulating, removed (and if they have, it's because their parents have made them like that). Does that sound like the sort of person you want to be?

Playful people are productive people. If we are enjoying what we do, we are inclined to do more of it.

■ Learn to utilize your 'child mind' when you need to

We never lost it. It just got hidden under the 24-hours-a-day adults we have now become. Buried there somewhere is our curiosity, our experimental side, our need for variety and life enrichment. We still get excited (and apprehensive) at the possibilities of the new, but often choose to play safe or ignore the myriad opportunities we have.

■ Work is serious...but you don't need to be

The problem-solver is not the person who ties themselves up in emotional knots over the problem. A separation of 'me' from the problems and challenges that the workplace throws up puts us psychologically in a better position to come up with the solutions.

By inclination we find it easier to explore and 'play' with the things that we think won't do us harm. However, the number of us willing to play when the degree of unknowns increases drops rapidly. The serious situation demands 'seriousness'. And yet it's that seriousness building up inside us that can hinder us as we deal with these unknowns. The seriousness makes us less able to keep the mind open and balanced enough to deal with new and challenging situations. The person who copes with the crisis is the one who keeps a cool head – who takes the situation seriously but themselves lightly. We see great examples of the benefit of this calmness in the way aid workers operate in human catastrophes such as the 2004 Asian tsunami. Even in the most serious situation, being calm and controlled works best.

Recognize the positive effects of a playful mentality. Taking your work seriously needn't mean being 'serious'.

■ Remove false barriers

One of the biggest barriers to adopting a more playful mentality at work is the assumption that the organization we work for actually exists. Organizations are no more than collections of individuals. If we believe that the organization is a barrier, we immediately put ourselves in a position of powerlessness because we cannot 'change' the organization. If we believe that the organization is its people, we are in a stronger position because we can always work to improve our relationships with people.

■ Be natural

There aren't many of us who don't want to enjoy ourselves at work. On the other hand, most of us don't want to be told how to enjoy ourselves (see 'Do what comes naturally' below). We want to be free to express ourselves in our unique ways. We all have multi-dimensional personalities, but we learn to utilize the parts that will work best for us in any given situation. We remain true to ourselves.

■ Choice

You can choose how you approach your work. We have no choice about working. We do have a choice about playing. The variable here is whether we want to play – are we motivated to want to enjoy our work more? Motivated people go to work to 'play'. Unmotivated people go to 'work'.

Remember that no matter what work you do, you can always choose the attitude you have while you do that work.

■ Novelty

As human beings we need novelty to keep us stimulated. Being playful creates novelty because the playful mind is a curious one and curiosity opens up new opportunities. Try to balance the routine with the new.

■ You are replaceable

Hey, what's a negative statement doing in a book on positive thinking? The answer is realism – many of us are replaceable. In most working environments we are forgotten six months after we've gone. We owe it to ourselves to access the fun or joy from any situation in which we find ourselves. It's not healthy to lower our own standards when we can hold our head high and tell the world, 'I know how to enjoy myself'.

■ Do what comes naturally

What playing at work isn't:
■ Dress-down Friday.
■ Play-Doh in meetings.
■ Organized 'fun' activities.
■ A feeling that you can't be yourself.

What playing at work is:

- Being yourself.
- Not being afraid to be yourself.
- Being spontaneous.
- Bringing colleagues in on the enjoyment you are having.
- Not feeling like you are 'working'.
- Feeling comfortable saying 'I don't want to play today'.

Playful organizations do not exist. That is because, as we have seen, organizations do not exist. Playful people exist everywhere. The more playful people we have, the more fun our work can be. You can be one of the people who choose to play. But we cannot rely on our employer to create the conditions for us where we are able to play. Many of us will be waiting for a very long time. If we want to enjoy ourselves more at work – to play, to have fun, to be ourselves – the energy for this will come only from each of us.

> **It's down to you!**
> *Being 'playful' at work has very little to do with the organizations we work for and everything to do with the way we approach our work.*

■ Getting into the 'flow'

Sometimes workers are able to engage so deeply in their 'work' that they forget they are actually working. They 'flow', moving from position A to position B in an almost ethereal manner, without recourse to extreme emotion or stress, and seem to love what they are doing.

Try this exercise: think of a time when you were really enjoying your job.

1 How would you describe how you felt?
2 What made it so enjoyable?

Our answers to Question 1 may have included otherworldly, lost in what I was doing, challenged, confident and maybe even exhilarated. Our answers to Question 2 may have included no barriers (or I was so engaged I didn't notice them), highly productive, time flew by, unstressed, enjoying myself (on reflection) and fulfilled. Sometimes the answers to both questions will be the same.

These are all characteristics of what psychologist Mike Csikszentmihalyi calls our state of flow – a higher plane of working that we gravitate to when we are truly engaged with what we do. Our answers to Question 1 give us a sense of what the state of flow feels like. Our answers to Question 2 give us the benefits.

Think about what gives a river life. A river that doesn't flow, where the water is still, struggles to support life. The water goes stagnant and there is little oxygen for living things to survive. Everything eventually rots. A river that flows takes in oxygen and supports an abundance of life – fish, plants and amphibians. It's the same with us at work. Get into the state of flow and we create in ourselves a highly productive, energetic, engaged person. In addition, we are more likely to create that feeling in others because our positivity rubs off. Never getting into flow means we stagnate, remain unchallenged and see work as a grind.

Being in a state of flow means we lose our sense of time because our engagement with what we are doing makes time irrelevant. We get so lost in what we are doing that we lose an awareness of anything outside what it is we are doing. We've all experienced this at work, but probably more when we were enjoying a hobby. This is the point when play becomes 'flow'. The idea that we are working doesn't enter our head.

There are some things we can do to get ourselves to that flow state more often:

■ Creating purpose
If you've created your own work-related GOATs based on the SMARTER chart on page 183, you are more likely to experience flow states – provided you really want to achieve those GOATs. Desire is key.

Define a purpose in your work – no matter what the work is.

■ Keeping curious
Asking 'How can I do this better?' or 'Why do we do it that way?' and acting on the answers gets us closer to control over our work. People in 'flow' feel in control.

▧ Making a difference

If what we are doing makes a real difference and we can see the impact of that difference, we put more in. If what you do makes no difference, why are you doing it?

▧ Being an 'intrapreneur'

Anyone who successfully works for themselves will experience 'flow' often. Those who don't are unlikely to be working for themselves for long. We positive thinkers who are employees can get to a state of flow by beginning to see ourselves as the 'company of one' – even when we are employed. Imagine that you don't really work for the organization that employs you at the moment. Or rather you do, but not in the way that you currently do. Imagine yourself as the 'intrapreneur' whose success is dependent on your own sense of pride in your work and your desire to have strong relationships with colleagues and customers.

These are things that are crucial to entrepreneurs and self-employed people. Their livelihood depends on it. That level of engagement with the work we do and the people we do it with gets us 'flowing'.

▧ Learning new skills

When we learn new skills we want to put them into practice. Feeling that we are developing as a person creates a closer engagement with our work. We are answering the WIIFM (what's in it for me?) question, so we engage better with the things that give us benefits.

▧ Know thyself

As we've seen throughout this book, self-awareness is a trait of nearly all positive thinkers. Positive thinkers don't use 'the job wasn't right for me' as an excuse for inertia because we give our best in any situation. But we can make an assessment of the kind of job that is going to sit best with our personality. We do need to be honest with ourselves. The glamour pursuits (say, in more creative worlds) are right for some of us and very wrong for others, but it can be tempting to go for the image rather than the reality of work in the creative field. We can end up very unhappy if we push ourselves into a world that isn't right for us.

What sort of working environment suits you best? Look at the suggestions below and write down a score for each out of 10 according to what you think you are suitable for – 10 being a perfect fit down to 1 being a complete mismatch.

1 Intra/entrepreneurial
Where a lot of personal space is required to let our natural energy shine through. Sales and running a business are good examples.
Score:

2 Communal
Where we want to be close to the worlds of others. Social workers, charity workers and less egocentric politicians fall into this category.
Score:

3 Cerebral
Where our need for intellectual pursuits dealing in both abstract and creative spheres is fulfilled. Teachers and scientific researchers often live in this world.
Score:

4 Creative
These jobs are occupied by those of us who seek to bring the world of our own imagination into the physical world in which we live. Musicians, graphic designers and computer games developers are among the obvious examples.
Score:

5 Practical
Where we like to operate in controlled environments with explicit GOATs. Construction workers, engineers and farmers are good examples.
Score:

6 Conformist
Where a need to work within the rules – and where the rules are not continually reinterpreted – is fulfilled. Finance and accountancy suit this person.
Score:

7 Free spirit

Where we need a high degree of personal space beyond the creative, intra/entrepreneurial level. More bohemian lifestyles sit here.

Score:

Adapted from J.L. Holland, *Making Vocational Choices*

Take a look at your scores and reflect on whether you are in the right job for you – or if you need a better match between your personality and your job. Honesty is important for us because part of being positive about our work comes from being positive about our choice of work. That said, before we make the change from one career path to another we need to assess if the problems we have are down to our own attitude to our work or to a mismatch between ourselves and the work we do. We can probably name many people who just had a bad attitude and no amount of job changing was going to make it better for them until they addressed the problem within.

Remember that it is never too late to change direction. We get one life and it's very sad if we spend around 80,000 hours of it doing something that isn't right for us.

> *Problems with the job?*
> *Positive thinkers ask: Is the problem me or the job?*
> *Positive thinkers look to 'me' first.*

Is there such a thing as a 'boring' job?

Many readers are likely to have seen the energizing *Fish!* video – one of the most successful corporate training videos ever made. In the film we witness a real team of 12 people working on a cold, smelly fish stall at Pike Place Fish Market in Seattle. This is nobody's idea of a dream job, yet through energy, passion, commitment and the simple act of throwing fish around the stall ('Beware flying fish' posters adorn the walls) and providing a 'show' for the public, the workers there have transformed what to many would be a spectacularly boring working environment into a fun place to be. A huge crowd watches them 'at work', hoping some of the energy rubs off on them.

As one of the workers says: 'Twelve-hour days just fly by.' As well as 'flying' they're 'flowing'! Johnny Yokohama, the boss of the fish stall, reminds viewers that 'We're not working, we're playing.' Much of what they do could be seen as routine – selling fish, taking money and so on – but somehow they have made the leap from routine to dream.

'But this is my world...'

We must acknowledge that there are circumstances that challenge even the most positive thinker. Perennial change – to the point where we feel that any positive input we give to our job is immediately rubbed out by the next 'initiative', merger or newly arrived chief executive (workers the world over will relate to this) – can make us feel impotent.

In these environments we can take ourselves in different directions. We can complain about our ever-changing circumstances to the point of inertia and probably bring down those around us well. We can 'hoe our row' and hope nobody really notices. Many of us may just choose to drift, to disengage psychologically from what we do and hope to get through to retirement without too many other troubles on the way. That is an individual choice. But it isn't the right choice for a positive thinker. Drift is alien territory.

Younger readers who feel unchallenged in their job can still choose to engage 'whole...heart...head...ly' in an unchallenging job on the basis that we are climbing the ladder and investing in something that maybe we don't particularly enjoy but where we can see long-term benefit in sticking with it. By creating a clear purpose here we are creating the circumstances that are likely to get us out of the unchallenging role into something more rewarding.

Some of us make the decision that our work is merely a means to an end. The things that many others get from work we get from our outside pursuits, and we're happy with that. We may feel we have only so much to give and choose to give it to out-of-hours voluntary work, to a sports club or to bringing up our children. That is a positive choice. Who are we to criticize?

Choice

When we come down to it there are very few of us who don't want to play, to be in flow, to be in a job that we enjoy. The key question is: how much do we really want those things? If we want them enough, we will find them. If they are simply idle wishes, they will probably remain just that. The responsibility sits with each of us to be positive about our work. It really is down to you!

■ Living through change

Change, and our capacity to deal with it, is a subject that could probably sit in almost any of the chapters in this book. It's included here because changes in our working circumstances are a central feature of our working life. US citizens are known to joke that you are unemployable if you haven't been made redundant at least once! However, much of what is written in this section relates to changes that are or will be taking place in our whole life and not just our work. The examples here are taken from a wide spectrum of living.

It is easy to say positive thinkers react positively to change, but not particularly helpful if we are feeling isolated, out of control and bereft of direction. What can be helpful is to have a sense of why we are reacting the way we are, and to understand how we can get to a position of acceptance quickly. From this position of acceptance we are more able to think rationally and lay out a plan of action. The key is not that we have negative thoughts when confronted with change – these thoughts are entirely natural – but that we get to a position where we can respond positively as quickly as possible.

To begin with, it can be useful to have an understanding of how we, as individuals, react to change in our life – or at least to get a clearer reading of our own instinctive reaction to change. Understanding our own reaction to change increases our capacity to deal with it. In the Personal resources section at the end of this book there is a questionnaire (Exercise 4, page 187) that will help you take your own change reading. The questionnaire was devised by Philip Hodson, who is head of the British Society of Psychotherapists as well as a prolific writer and broadcaster. The questionnaire takes around ten minutes to complete. It links to the change cycle section below, but it is not essential to do it if you want to read on.

The change cycle

Philip Hodson has identified four key dimensions in the change cycle: negation, self-justification, exploration and resolution. They can be positioned in a change cycle as shown in the diagram overleaf:

The four dimensions

As a simple exercise, start by writing down two headings: 'Current changes' and 'My reaction'. Identify some changes that you are going through and write them down under 'Current changes'. Examples might include: new boss at work, moving house, new job and so on. Try not to include just the things that on the face of it fill you with apprehension. It may be that happy events, such as having a baby, getting an unexpected cash windfall or winning promotion may well stir similar 'apprehension-like' emotions anyway – in many situations our initial reaction may not correlate with the potential of the new situation, even when we are aware of that potential. Then under 'My reaction' write a few single words that summarize how you feel.

Many of these words are likely to be emotive and indeed, when confronted with change, we are likely to use emotive language to deny that the change is occurring – 'It's not really happening' or 'I can't believe it' are typical comments when we are in this dimension. When we do this we are in the negation phase.

It's an interesting paradox that the very things we often crave in our work – variety, new challenges and job enrichment – are also the things that can bring us initial feelings of discomfort. At the same time the threat of change in our working circumstances – possible redundancy, reorganization, merger, takeover, new boss and so on – can provoke very real and very natural negative reactions in us. It's important to remember that negative emotions are entirely natural in the most positive of thinkers. Most of us would be justified in having very negative emotions bordering on fear if we suspected we were about to lose our job. On the other hand, this initial negativity can become highly toxic if we choose to wallow in it for too long. After a time the negativity will get us nowhere and may begin to affect our mental and physical well-being.

In the second dimension (self-justification) we find reasons to justify our denial. We hide ourselves away and pretend this change is not happening. Hide for long enough and it will go away. But when we poke our head out we realize it is still there.

Positive thinking in these circumstances means coming to terms with our changed circumstances in a realistic timeframe so that we can move forward more quickly. Just jumping in – 'This is the chance I have been looking for' – can be good, but sometimes we need to consider the impact and our possible responses so that we can maximize positive aspects of the change. If we carry this kind of thinking with us, we are likely to move into the final two phases, exploration and resolution, more quickly.

When we move to exploration we move into a positive realm. Accepting that the change is here, we begin to look for possibilities. It is possible to survive in a kind of limbo between self-justification and exploration. We have all met people who seem to hanker after the past with little real commitment to the future. This is a 'survive' rather than 'thrive' mentality.

Finally we move into resolution – we say to ourselves, 'This what I am going to do'. The positive thinking of the exploration phase turns into the positive action of the resolution phase.

The challenge for us is to move positively to a position of acceptance and positive action as quickly as we can. As positive thinkers, we see ourselves as explorers – looking for the opportunities through the opening up of our imagination. And as positive thinkers we resolve to take action rather than just think about taking action.

Proactivity – the fifth dimension

As valuable as these four dimensions are, there is a fifth dimension that sits over the whole change cycle – and, in fact, when we get it right pre-empts it. In earlier chapters we discussed our capacity for psychological travel and for opportunity-spotting. These are proactive mental (and sometimes physical) processes that allow us to see a variety of futures. We create options for ourselves. The best way to deal with change is to create it ourselves. The proactive approach does this for us.

Sarah's story

I had been in my job as a receptionist a long time – about ten years. The job wasn't bad at all – I enjoyed being at the front of the company, seeing new faces every day, and I had quite a bit to do. It had never really crossed my mind to change jobs. I mean, we all joke about it, but 12 months later only a handful of faces have changed. Then suddenly the worst thing (at that time) happened to me. The company announced that it was merging with another one to form a single larger company. I knew what it meant right away and I was devastated. We were moving to the site of the company we were merging with (they were the bigger partner) and guess what? They would need only one receptionist! I had no idea what to do really, I was in such a panic, so I didn't do very much to begin with.

For the next month or so not much happened – the move was to take place in two months from the announcement. By then I knew I was being made redundant, but it was easy to believe that nothing was happening, and I have to say I didn't do very much to get a new job. About a week before I was meant to go I hit panic mode. The realization hit me that this really was for real.

It took me about a month to get another job. The new job wasn't in reception at all – I was working in an office in an administrative role for a big insurance company. After a while interesting things started to happen. Recognizing that I had pretty good organizational skills, my new employer – I won't name them but you will have heard of them – started to give me more responsibility. I started to manage other people as well, something I'd never really even thought about. Right now I'm an office manager controlling resources and taking responsibility for lots of different people. I earn a lot more than I did before as well, which is nice.

When I was made redundant I thought it was a disaster. It made me do something I would never have done. I was incredibly stale, a bit bored and probably being taken advantage of in my old job. Five years on, I feel a part of me which I didn't really think existed has been allowed to express itself. The change has been a breath of fresh air, possibly the best thing that has ever happened to me. It didn't feel like it at the time, though!

Order in chaos

One characteristic of those who seem to exist on a diet of relentless change in their personal and professional life is that they often seem to need a part of their life to give them stability. As long ago as 1970, Alvin Toffler recognized this in his book *Future Shock*, talking of stability zones and illustrating the point with stories of people who appear to have parts of their life in chaos (multiple affairs, new job every year and so on), but who have another part of their life in complete order – regimented waking-up routine, for example. This knowledge can be quite useful in helping us to understand where our stability zones exist and where we leave space for growth and risk. It is likely that if change hits our stability zone, we may well find it harder to move round the change cycle we worked with earlier (page 159). If change happens in our 'risk' zone, we may feel very comfortable with it because we have already selected the change option as a lifestyle choice in this aspect of our life. However, we should beware here too. If, for example, we like travelling as part of our work and enjoy the changes this brings, we will find it tough if it is taken from us.

Below is a stability/growth/risk chart for a person I know (not me!). Why not have a go at developing your own? It may help you to understand where change is likely to be at its most sensitive for you.

Stability zone	Growth zone	Risk zone
Personal friendships	Likes young people	Numerous affairs
Career	Listens	Likes to shock
Her home	Social	
Lived in the same city for most of life	Open-minded	
▼	▼	▼
Change at its most challenging	Change is likely to be frustrating	Change is the norm

Change that hits the stability zone of our example above is likely to be the most painful. Change that hits the growth zone is likely to be frustrating as the person enjoys socializing and might find it challenging if that avenue of adventure were cut off. The risk zone is interesting. Broken relationships are likely to have led to heartache, but also to have provided experience in coming to terms with losses. New relationships are part of life's currency for this person. All models have holes, and there are some here – there will be many exceptions to the rule – but it does provide a useful tool to help 'know thyself' and, as a result, to better understand our reaction to change.

Of course there are many who live their life in the stability zone, possibly because of fear of change. On the other hand, having experienced enforced change and deciding it wasn't as bad as they thought it might be, they might be a little more adventurous in future. Some, however, may be chastened for life and hide in their metaphorical shell as much as possible.

I am as I am

In Chapter 4, 'Tuning in', we looked at the importance of self-knowledge in helping us to think in a more positive way. The exercises outlined in this chapter are designed to help us increase our awareness of how and why we react to change in the way we do. The challenge is to use this as a base point from which we can learn to embrace change quickly, not as a point of no return. Saying 'I am as I am' shuts the door to the possibility that, along with your circumstances changing, you can change too. If we want to be more positive, it is essential that we are flexible enough as individuals to recognize that we can adapt.

We've heard people say, 'Nothing exciting ever happens to me'. Is it because those who say this never do anything exciting? If they think that nothing exciting ever happens to them, they are also telling themselves that that's the reality of their personality and therefore their life (I am as I am). In this case, they aren't likely to do much to change their circumstances so that exciting things do happen to them. In fact, they may have convinced themselves that this is an undeniable reality to the point where they would not recognize opportunities for excitement anyway. 'Nothing ever happens to me' becomes the perfect self-fulfilling prophecy. Change creates the excitement that many of us crave. Sometimes we need to go through the insecurity and denial to get to the excitement and action. Sometimes we never get there. Sometimes we go straight to action.

It can be helpful to look at children and how they react to change. Children's reactions to most things are explicit. When we move into adulthood we are more inclined to keep our feelings bottled up – even though our internalized feelings often leak out. Children may have the same or perhaps deeper feelings of insecurity. They may seek comfort or reassurance from parents. They may just say 'no'. Adults are rarely as direct. Parents will, however, recognize how a child can jump from complete refusal to do something to complete immersion in that self-same thing a few moments later if they suddenly see the possibility of fun, learning and adventure. It's 'Parents get out of the way – my playground just got bigger!' It's that connection between the new and the possibilities of the new that we need to make if we are to maximize the value of changed circumstances.

▓ It's all in the timing

We've all met remarkably productive people who don't feel the need to work before 8.45 a.m. or after about 5.15 p.m. And we've all met people who apparently live at the office and seem to achieve very little. If we really are 'playing for a living', we might not object to being 'at work' all the time, but positive thinkers value balance and variety in their life. Too much living in one dimension of life, no matter how initially rewarding, can lead to mental sterility, narrow thinking and ultimately lower productivity. So maybe it's not beneficial to be working until nine o'clock at night – and are we really productive when we're into the 13th hour of our working day?

Many writers – who can often choose when they write – start at six or seven in the morning because, even though they've just got out of bed, they report that the clarity of thinking required is heightened at that time. Many also report that the brilliant piece of prose they thought they were composing late at night turns out the next morning to be nonsense.

Try some of these time tips:

■ Set team 'time standards'

Most of us don't work in a personal cocoon. We have to interact with teammates, colleagues and other departments all through the day. This is the chance for the positive thinker to act as initiator. Can we organize it so that each of us gets an hour of undisturbed time in a day? Can we put a time limit on meetings? What's our email protocol?

■ Tackle the tough tasks when your mind is freshest

Although it may not always seem that way, studies show that most us are at our most productive in the earlier part of the day. Using the morning to its full potential opens up the possibilities of the afternoon when perhaps we can indulge in the parts of the job compatible with our mental condition. Our day won't always work out the way we want it to, but we can try to utilize our freshness to personal advantage.

■ Do first the thing you least like doing – eat 'brains for breakfast'

Few of us would find eating brains pleasant at any time of the day, least of all when we've just got up. The gurus of managing our time tell us that planning and prioritizing are crucial – but hey! – there's nothing like getting the thing you least like doing out of the way good and early. Putting it off means that the guilt 'dances' at the back of the mind all day because the worst is yet to come. The things that we enjoy doing aren't so pleasurable because we know we've got something less enjoyable still to do.

■ Vary the routine

It's not always possible, if your job really is of the one-dimensional variety (note to positive-thinking managers – create variety in your team's work, share the less enjoyable tasks around), but try to vary your routine. For example, heavy computer users can end up letting the computer control them, so set time aside to get away from the screen. Go and talk to people.

But we can be creative about how we see our working day. We can create variety in the way we get to work, how we spend our lunchtime, how we get home (see page 169 for more on this) if our job involves long hours performing similar tasks. Or even if it doesn't.

■ Make a note of any random but inspirational thoughts that strike you – don't lose them

Great ideas can hit us at the moment we least expect them and we're good at congratulating ourselves on the insight, going off to do something else and then forgetting the idea. We scratch around for the idea we had, but the harder we try to locate it in the mind, the less able we are to access it. Carry a notebook with you, write it on the back of your hand, have a graffiti board above your desk. You don't need to perfect the idea – 'don't get it right, get it written' is the old maxim.

■ Don't kill off the morning's potential with a three-hour meeting

Maybe we should expand that by saying don't have a meeting that lasts three hours at any time of the day! We've got all that freshness in the room, all that energy. All of it being crushed. While we are in a meeting we aren't doing anything. We're just talking about doing things. Or more often than not talking ourselves out of doing things. Keep the meeting short and focused on action. Positive meetings create positive actions.

■ Why waste the precious first hour of the day on routine emails?

Hey, aren't you the popular one – 120 emails in the inbox this morning! Let's spend the next two hours answering them all. This most glorious of communication tools has become in its short life one of biggest barriers to successful communication through misuse. There are lots of email-management systems to help us filter out the good from the bad but still we find ourselves overloaded. Some things never change. Twenty years ago we were complaining about the mountain of paper in the in-tray. Now it's relocated to the computer screen.

Just occasionally it is OK for a positive thinker to be a pain. Keep your standards high. We can let it be known that we won't accept personal action points given by others that have been copied to us. We can let it be known that we still value conversation and that receiving an email request from someone sitting at the next desk is not really acceptable. And on top of that we can think about the best way of challenging people (without damaging our relationship) who continually send us emails 'because you might be interested'. They are often trying to protect themselves and pass the buck to us by saying: 'Well, I told you.'

Priority emails deserve the utmost priority. The routine can be saved for quieter times.

■ Playing 'Space Invaders'

The 'Space Invader' is the unwanted visitor who wants to have a 45-minute conversation at 9.05 a.m. about how much they had to drink last night or their success or otherwise as a Lothario-type character from *Sex and the City*. Being sociable is great – there's nothing more dispiriting for the whole team than the ice-cold efficiency expert who has no personal warmth in them. However, turning the office into the bar is not so good – particularly if we want to go home at night. Of course it doesn't need to be a social conversation. The Space Invader who wants to talk about a work-related issue at a time that is inconvenient to us has to be 'deflected' in a way that does no damage to our relationship.

Leadership expert John Adair came up with 'Be ruthless with time and gracious with people' as a guiding principle when chatter is encroaching on our day. In another great piece of advice he said that if the Space Invader is beginning to outstay their welcome, consider 'perching on the end of the desk'. It sends a subliminal signal that we want the meeting/discussion to be short and that we have somewhere else to go to.

■ Breaking habits

When we join a new company we're in the honeymoon period. We're feeling enthusiastic, ambitious, confident (because we've had affirmation of our abilities), nervous and excited. For the most part your colleagues will be pleased that you have joined them. Most will want some of your positive energy to rub off on them, while making sure that you know 'This is the way we do it!'

But over time things change. We find it difficult to maintain the emotional peak of our honeymoon period and find ourselves operating within the rigidity of the existing structure. But this can be as much about having a frame of mind that gets lodged in routine as it is about the job. We looked at breathing freshness into our life in Chapter 6 (page 121). There are many aspects of work we can't change, including certain tasks and the people around us. There are things we can try to do as positive people to address this, and they both involve flicking a personal switch that helps us to see the routine in a different way.

What we can do is ask ourselves how we can break routine and look at performing these run-of-the-mill tasks in a different way. Learning to 'play' at work helps us do so, but this process starts before we even get to work. Why not change the way you travel to work tomorrow? City dwellers have lots of options. You could go by yourself or with a friend, you could walk or cycle, go by quad-bike, on a train, river-bus, helicopter, aeroplane, hang-glider or rickshaw. Or you could parachute in, hitch-hike, swim or water-ski. Non-urban dwellers have choices too. How about travelling by horse? Camel? Elephant? Too ridiculous? Maybe for you (and only maybe) – but remember the worlds of others may be very different from your own.

Try reading a different newspaper/magazine/book while you travel. Reading the same newspaper every day can leave you open to one-track thinking – the track that the newspaper editor wants you to be on.

Read a right-wing newspaper? Try a left-wing one tomorrow. How can you be sure of your own world-view if you don't know the world-view of those who disagree with you?

Try to change the routine you have built around your work even when you're not actually at work if you find yourself getting stale.

■ Nobody's choice but mine

A continuing life theme for positive thinkers is 'choice'. The choices available to us come in two forms:

■ Recognizing the choices we have as we go through life.
■ Recognizing that we can choose the attitude we bring to any situation.

Choice applies equally to our work. The motivational storyteller Carr Hagerman talks of coming across an organization in the USA where, by reception, there is a big wall displaying badges. On the badges are written words that describe the different kinds of attitude we could have that day – happy, sad, angry, reflective, tired and so on. Staff are encouraged to take one that reflects their mood that morning as they come into work.

We can only imagine where this exercise in better understanding of each other went (and that's what I assume they did it for – I could be wrong), but it's possible that individuals would very quickly start to pick a badge that reflects the mood they would like to have that day. Or that some of the more enterprising act up to the badge that they decided to wear.

This issue of choosing a badge teaches us a lot about choice. If we are conscious of 'wearing' an attitude (even if it is the one we are actually feeling) we become much more conscious of the effect of that attitude both on ourselves and on those around us.

Try this exercise yourself for a week: copy the chart below on to a sheet of paper and monitor the effect both on yourself and others.

Attitude chart

	Attitude a.m.	Effects	Attitude p.m.	Effects
Monday	_____	_____	_____	_____
Tuesday	_____	_____	_____	_____
Wednesday	_____	_____	_____	_____
Thursday	_____	_____	_____	_____
Friday	_____	_____	_____	_____

The next week, rather than working with the attitude you are feeling, try to pick one. I've suggested some below: first the attitude, then the behaviour that comes out of that attitude and then the result of that behaviour.

Attitude	Behaviour	Result
Curious	Questioning	Learning
Happy	Warm	Infectious happiness
'Chilled'	Relaxed	Unstressed
Passive	Unassertive	Taken advantage of
Assertive	Honest, open	Results!

Of course, do add some of your own. 'Creative', 'involving', 'sharing' and 'confident' are good examples of ones you might like to use. The key here is to choose to behave in a way that is productive. Being conscious of the attitude you have will make you more conscious of the effect of it.

There is a famous saying, 'Behaviour breeds behaviour', which is another way of saying that you get what you give. Grunt at someone when they say good morning and don't be surprised if they don't bother the next day.

Even if you don't wear a badge (and I wouldn't blame you if you didn't), be conscious of your attitude each day and of how it changes during that day. There are days when we just 'snap out of it' if it's unproductive, and days when we don't want to lose it if it's a good one.

■ Working positively

Some readers who perhaps have attended rather too many training courses for their own liking may wonder why subjects such as managing your time and dealing with change appear in a book like this. The answer, as many readers may be thinking, is that seeing work in a positive way impacts on all aspects of our job. Managing time, for example, is one of the biggest challenges facing us at work, and approaching our working day in a positive manner – right from the start of it – helps us get the job done.

So to summarize: we have no choice about going to work, but we do have a choice about the way we do it; we can choose to let work be something that happens to us, or we can choose to make the effort to enjoy it as much as we can.

Do I happen to the job or does the job happen to me?

In any moment of decision the best thing you can do is the right thing, the next best is the wrong thing, and the worst is nothing.

Theodore Roosevelt

Chapter 8
Controlling the heat

❏ Temperature control

❏ The fullness of life

❏ The energy of beginning

■ Temperature control

A running theme in this book is that our ability to think positively takes the flame that exists within each of us and turns it into a powerful internal heater that drives us forward. But what would happen if we lost control of the heating system? Our capacity to act positively gets stretched to the point where we believe we have become the centre of the universe.

To make sure that an effective system does not run amok, I suggest two mechanisms for emotional temperature control: preservation of integrity and controlling of ego. You may be asking: Why reserve a special place in the conclusion of the book for these two things? The reason is that one of the core themes of this book is that as positive thinkers we try to give more to the world than we take from it. We leave a net benefit. There are many out there who could be described by some as positive thinkers but whose lack of integrity and over-inflated ego do more damage than good. Maintaining our integrity and controlling our ego keep us on the right side.

Keeping our integrity

Here is a dilemma:

You are riding in a car driven by a close friend. He hits a pedestrian. You know he was going at least 35 mph in an area where the maximum speed allowed is 20 mph. There are no witnesses. His lawyer says that if you testify under oath that he was driving at only 20 mph, it might save him from serious consequences. What right has your friend to expect you to protect him?

Fons Trompenaars and Charles Hampden Turner, *Riding the Waves of Culture*

What in your mind would be the moral position to take? How would you preserve your integrity? Could you preserve your integrity in this situation?

Here are some possible responses:

1 My friend has a definite right to expect me to testify to the lower figure.
2 He has some right as a friend to expect me to testify to the lower figure.
3 He has no right as a friend to expect me to testify to the lower figure.

So in the light of answering 1, 2 or 3, would you testify that he was doing 20 mph or not?

Fons Trompenaars uses this dilemma to point up cultural differences. Our preference for saying whether our friend was doing 20 mph or not depends on whether we have a preference for relationships or rules: these preferences are often born out of cultural norms.

Here I am using it to introduce the topic of integrity because our cultural background plays a key part in determining whether we make a decision that protects our integrity. There would, of course, be no global consensus on what the 'right' decision is, partly because there is no satisfactory description of what integrity is. It's a nebulous term open to wide interpretation.

So with all the vagueness (which I freely admit!), why are we debating it here? This raises another dilemma – but one that is easier to answer. If we assess the character traits of Adolf Hitler or Pol Pot or, indeed, of a 'snake-oil' salesman, we could say that many of them fall in line with the characteristics of positive thinkers highlighted so far in this book. Integrity can also be a character trait of positive thinkers (and, in a perverse way, of despots), yet not many readers (I hope none) would describe these people as role models.

Clearly, morality is key, and we can argue strongly that positive-thinking readers maintain integrity based on moral considerations. Defining morality, however, poses the same problems as defining integrity. Is it enough to say that we need to take a moral stance to maintain our integrity? It may have to be. As with many other things, we know a person who has integrity when we see one. We may have to look at ourselves in the metaphorical mirror here.

We move outside the realm of positive thinking in the next section but not outside the realm of positive action. Living in 'freer' societies gives us a wide arc in which to express ourselves, but the framework below may help in deciding whether our actions encroach beyond what would be considered acceptable behaviour in modern society. This book takes a strong standpoint in arguing that maintenance of integrity and respect for the values of the global society in which we live are essential parts of our makeup as positive thinkers. Here is a framework to help positive thinkers maintain integrity in their actions.

■ Tolerance

Defined here as 'live and let live', but has its basis in giving people the freedom to live their life as they wish provided they don't harm others. Manifestations of this include religious and racial tolerance. Different religions have their own convergent set of moral values beyond the scope of the list on this page. Some of the Ten Commandments central to Christianity are included (Thou shalt not kill, steal, etc.), others are more debatable (Thou shalt not commit adultery, for example).

■ Trust
Honesty, trustworthiness and respect for others can be included here.

■ The primacy (and flexibility) of law
Crucial to the stability of 'rule-based' societies. It's ironic that societies with the most freedom also have the most clearly defined legislative framework and respect for the law.

■ Respect for the property of others
Manifests itself as a respect for personal space. This is a key one because wealthy Western economic systems depend on the value of property and property rights as the basis for their stability. We are deeply protective of this without necessarily realizing it.

■ A reasonable morality that does not harm others
This is a tough one. Some have argued that capitalist systems are harmful and that what one describes as capitalist pursuits with the accent on the 'self' are damaging to the world as a whole. Others (and one must say the majority in many modern/modernizing societies) feel the opposite.

Do readers agree that what one does in the privacy of one's own home is nobody else's business as long as it does no harm to others?

■ A framework that can remind individuals when they are acting immorally
Law, free press and free speech are key components here.

Controlling the urge
A great piece of advice to help maintain integrity is to learn to control emotion-based, impulsive actions that we might regret later. We often learn

this through experience. A bill with mistakes in it comes through the letterbox and we're immediately on the phone to the service provider, venting our fury. We often end up embarrassed at our loss of control and learn that a rational, calm approach yields results. Learn to identify those situations where you may potentially lose control or make irrational decisions. Don't let emotion hijack reason. Positive thinking fans the flames of your internal fire. Maintaining integrity ensures that the fire does not get out of control.

Controlling the ego

Some way down the line, perhaps in a few years' time, we're succeeding in the things we want to but the warning light comes on. It's warning about the (perhaps overstated) appearance of our ego. The ego is something that appears when we are trying to hide or suppress our true self. It's a veneer. An example of this is seen in superstars who start to believe all the publicity about them and forget who they really are. They start behaving to the image not the reality. We need to ask the question: Am I being true to my real self? Or, as Virginia Woolf once said, 'Am I telling the truth about myself?'

The key is to maintain our sense of perspective – to understand that 'I am the centre of my world, but I am not the centre of the 6 billion other worlds out there too.' And even if people treat us as though we are the centre of their world as well, only the foolish would believe in their own inflated sense of importance.

Take away the covering and remember who you really are.

■ The fullness of life

In 2001 author Laura Hillenbrand had a book published that featured the exploits of 1930s' racehorse superstar Seabiscuit and the team of terrific people who surrounded him. Laura Hillenbrand is a star too for bringing back to life a wonderful story that many but the oldest Americans were beginning to forget. I don't need to tell the story here but I recommend it as an inspiring read even if you don't like horses. The book tells a great tale of the full range of life's experiences – remarkable success, human endeavour, failure, sadness, illness, expertise, determination, optimism, intuition, self-belief and celebration. Reading it gave me a completely different take on what 'living your life' really means. Here we honour a great story with ten positive-thinking 'bites' to take away. We have explored all these themes in the book, so they can be seen as a handy summary of the book itself.

S   See the world through other sets of eyes
Look through the eyes of others for a different perspective. Take an umbrella view of the world and you'll see unlimited opportunity.

E   Engage your playful side at work
Bring the mentality you have 'at play' to your work. The benefits? You'll enjoy work more, you'll be more productive, you'll be less stressed. Take yourself lightly and your work seriously.

A   Ask what's good – focus on the positive
It's easy to pick out what didn't go so well. Try to pick out the good bits. What worked? What can I take with me that's positive? Ask what difference you can make next time through your own efforts.

B   Bring a great attitude with you
The better the attitude you have to your day, the better the chance of your day being a good one.

I   Imagine what success feels like
When working towards a specific GOAT, imagine yourself transported to the scene where you are succeeding. Feel the energy it gives you.

S   Seek pleasure and enjoyment – even in adversity
Life's meant to be enjoyed, so don't feel guilty about enjoying it. Even in the toughest moments find something you can enjoy.

C   Confront difficulties and challenges – don't ignore them
Putting off things we don't like doing or that are difficult for us inhibits our ability to enjoy the things we do like doing. The guilt 'dances' at the back of the mind. Problems don't go away.

U   Use it, don't lose it

All those positive emotions we have in us – optimism, humour, opportunity-spotting and so on – become harder to access the less we use them.

I   It's never too late to start...

The future is only one second away. What one thing could you do now to start your own positive-thinking journey?

T   Take personal responsibility for your successes and failures

Analyse your last success: what did you do that made the difference? Now think about your next challenge: what could you do to ensure success?

■ The energy of beginning

Positive thinking can help access the parts of us that lead to fulfilment of our emotional and spiritual needs, and those needs will be different for all of us. Positive thinking can provide us with the psychological dynamo we need to transport ourselves to the places we want to go to physically or mentally. The dynamo exists as a very powerful force in all of us – we can choose to suppress it or use it. Nothing in life is guaranteed, but we owe it to ourselves to give ourselves the best chance of getting to the places we want to get to, and positive thinking can help us throughout our personal journey. This book has tried to explain many of the thought processes that give us the chance to be active participants in our own life rather than watching our life pass by.

We've come too far to end it now...

If you've read much or all of this book, you really have come too far to end it now. The book may be finished, but your life isn't, and you can now choose to take your positive thoughts with you through the next stage of your life. You can turn those positive thoughts into positive actions or you can choose to forget them tomorrow. Try to action some of those future-focused exercises you did as you read the book.

It has been said that the most energetic word in the English language is 'begin'. The beginning starts when you close the last page of this book. Thank you for reading it.

Personal resources

■ Exercise 1 – Spotting and taking opportunities

To get a snapshot of your own potential for creating, spotting and taking opportunities, I have listed the following 21 statements. Simply put a cross or a tick next to each statement to indicate whether you agree or disagree with it. These are not black and white statements, so you may not find yourself feeling very strongly either way, but a cross or a tick would indicate a preference. Try to avoid putting the 'right' answer. Instead, be honest with yourself: don't just think of examples when you have applied the thinking to your own life – also think of times when you haven't.

1 Some opportunities are there for me for only a very short period of time. ☐
2 I know myself – sometimes opportunities need to be right for me. ☐
3 Sometimes the answer is right in front of me. ☐
4 I look for possibilities rather than waiting for them. ☐
5 My curiosity creates opportunities for me. ☐
6 I have multiple options – there is always more than one potential opportunity. ☐
7 Sometimes I need to break out of conventional wisdom. ☐
8 I am a realist – opportunities present obstacles too. ☐
9 Changes bring me opportunities. ☐
10 I'm less likely to see opportunity when I'm not looking. ☐
11 Routine can lead to less opportunity-spotting. I become the routine. ☐
12 If I let the lid off opportunities, I sometimes can't put it back on again – things have changed for ever. ☐

13 I've had great ideas – they just didn't seem that way at the time. ☐

14 Too much analysis – and I might talk myself out of it. ☐

15 I avoid using 'if only' statements – what's gone has gone. ☐

16 Learning new things creates possibilities for me. ☐

17 Opportunities can be created from my own imagination. ☐

18 I anticipate opportunities rather than reacting to them. ☐

19 I am as prepared as I can be to make the most of my opportunities. ☐

20 Opportunities may become problems if I don't act on them. ☐

21 I like the uncertainty that opportunity-taking can bring. ☐

Opportunity-spotting and -taking is loaded with ambiguity, so you may have found it difficult to put what you felt to be the 'right' answer anyway! But we can make a case for all 21 statements having some truth in them (although the thinking behind each statement will not apply in every situation), so if you have more than, say, 16 ticks, you are probably effective at generating, spotting and (possibly) acting on opportunities. Between 11 and 15 your personal opportunity currency is still positive, but you may be missing out in some areas or maybe you haven't had the experiences to make a judgement. Ten ticks or fewer and you may find that either you haven't had enough personal experiences to assess each of these statements in relation to your own life (because of your age, for example), or perhaps you aren't creating or spotting enough situations where opportunities present themselves. The crucial thing to remember is that all these statements will work for you *some of the time*. Back in Chapter 3 (page 63) we assess each of these statements and how they relate to our world of unparalleled opportunity.

■ Exercise 2 – Setting SMARTER GOATs

Opposite is a chart that will help you set your own GOATs. If you haven't yet read Chapter 5 on GOATs, you may find it useful to do so before you start to look at some of those you may want to set for yourself. In the chart are the two examples used in that chapter – taking up jogging to complete in a local road race, and learning to speak Chinese to a certain standard in five years. These are examples of short-term and long-term GOATs.

Setting SMARTER GOATs – a template for areas of development

	Speaking Chinese	Taking up jogging
Specific	5-minute conversation with Chinese person	Compete in local road race
Measure	A specific qualification	Complete 10 km (6 miles); possibly set a time target nearer the race itself
Action-based	1 x 2-hour lesson per week	30–60-minute jog per day
Realistic	Confirmed with tutor	Couple of practice jogs, plus technical info from internet
Timed/Review	30 July 2007, with interim milestones	In 4 months, with interim reviews
Purpose	Employment opportunities	Getting fit

Now over to you – why not try to set a SMARTER GOAT for yourself?

A reminder

Specific	What am I seeking to achieve?
Measurable	For example, quality standard
Action-based	What am I going to *do*?
Realistic	Subjective/researched/shared view on what is attainable
Timed/Reviewed	By when? Did I achieve what I set out to?

And are you energized by the GOAT you have set? Do you feel the fire burning a little more strongly inside? If you do – go for it. If you feel nothing, don't even try. A GOAT that doesn't interest or excite you is pointless. It's a question only you can answer.

■ Exercise 3 – Setting behavioural GOATs

Here is a powerful exercise taken and adapted from *The Dinosaur Strain* by Mark Brown – an excellent book that has been quoted already. This is a very personal exercise, which allows us to focus on some of the behavioural skills we can choose to develop as part of a rich and rewarding future. One of the great things about this exercise is its randomness. It takes us to parts of ourselves we may not have really thought about or explored before.

A worked example can be found below the GOAT grid (page 186) to help you in laying out your own.

Stage 1

As a starting point, list ten people below who have made a strong and lasting impression on you. You need not know personally all the people you list, but you do need to know a reasonable amount about them, and they should have had an influence on you, either positive or negative. They can be alive or dead.

To help you think about this, many who do this exercise choose relatives, teachers or an inspiring manager from early in their working life. In politically unstable countries it is not unusual for political figures to be chosen; for example, Slobodan Milosevic is clearly a major influence (albeit a negative one) to many Kosovo Albanians.

Make your list below (the order doesn't matter).

1 _____

2 _____

3 _____

4 _____

5 _____

6 _____

7 _____

8 _____

9 _____

10 _____

Stage 2

Having selected ten people, you are now in a position to attribute certain characteristics to them – with the help of the chart on page 186. Take the first three selections on your list. Find a characteristic that two of them share, and a second, different, characteristic for the third person. For example, it might be that the first and third person on your list are carefree, and that the second person is analytical (the characteristics do not need to be opposites). In that instance you would write 'carefree' on the dotted line on the left and 'analytical' on the dotted line on the right. When you've done this, go on to the next line for the fourth, fifth and sixth persons on your list and go through the same process. It's the randomness here that helps to make this exercise particularly interesting, so don't feel constrained by using the ranking numbers in the chart. Make up your own combinations of three people.

Stage 3

Once you have worked through six or seven combinations, you are now in a position to set personal GOATs. Your next task is to plot the point where you believe you are now. So if (using the above example) you believe yourself to be more carefree and less analytical, you will place an 'N' (for 'now') on the solid line in the middle, towards the left side. An 'N' placed at either extremity of that line indicates that you believe you have either a very strong carefree trait or a very strong analytical trait.

Stage 4

Once you've done this for five or six lines, you are now in a position to set some personal GOATs for different parts of your life. For example, you might wish to plot where you think your employer might like you to be. Using 'carefree/analytical' as our continuing example, if your work requires you to be highly analytical, place 'W' (for 'work') towards the right extremity. If a signifi-cant amount of freethinking is required (but not without a little analysis), your 'W' would be placed towards the left side but not at the extreme. An 'N' and a 'W' placed reasonably closely on a line indicate an attainable behavioural GOAT. A big gap may indicate that you are not in a job that fits you!

You can add extra dimensions to this. Are there behaviour traits that you want to develop? Why not plot 'PG' (for your 'personal goals') on each line to indicate where you would like to be. Again, big gaps may indicate unrealistic GOATs, so work within sensible parameters.

It is reasonable to say that while personalities may not change in the short to medium term, behaviour can, and this exercise provides a helpful method of making your behaviour appropriate for your current and/or future circumstances.

My personal GOAT grid

1, 2, 3 .... _____ ....

4, 5, 6 .... _____ ....

7, 8, 9 .... _____ ....

10, 1, 4 .... _____ ....

2, 5, 7 .... _____ ....

3, 6, 8 .... _____ ....

9, 10, 2 .... _____ ....

3 ,4, 9 .... _____ ....

1, 5, 8 .... _____ ....

10, 7, 6 .... _____ ....

Sample GOAT grid

   1 Muhammad Ali
   2 Mother
   3 Uncle Alf

1, 2, 3 ....Resilient........ PG   W   N _____ ....Flexible...........

In this example I have defined Muhammad Ali and Uncle Alf as resilient, and Mother as flexible. I have placed 'N' for 'Now' approximately in the middle.

The nature of my work ('W') requires a higher degree of resilience than I am currently displaying (I therefore have a work goal here). I am, however, a little concerned that in the future I will need to be more resilient because of potential changes I can see happening in my personal life ('PG' – personal goal), so I have a clear goal that relates to both my work and personal circumstances.

We are flying in the face of conventional wisdom that says that GOATs need to be measurable (see 'SMARTER GOATs', page 101). There is something rather distasteful (even if we could do it successfully) about measuring 'behaviour', and here we have to use gut feeling to decide if our behaviour is changing over time. On the basis that behaviour breeds behaviour, if you notice that the way others behave towards you changes and is more positive over time, you might feel that you are heading in the right direction.

There is a strong emphasis on your own personal values here, as well as recognition that we all have unique influences in our life that help to 'shape' us. Everyone's judgement grid will be different, and thus the influences on their life will be too. The importance of one aspect of psychological adventure – the capacity for 'interiority' – is made to resonate more strongly when we appreciate the huge diversity of people who comprise our world.

This also rather flies in the face of those personality profiles used in the workplace that attempt to reduce the people of the world to five or six personality types – often to help managers 'manage' us better. It perhaps isn't very helpful to encourage those of us who are managers to try to categorize those we manage when our job is more rewarding and productive if we can work with the uniqueness and individuality of all the team members. Likewise, as positive thinkers we embrace and celebrate the diversity of our 6 billion co-habitants – not categorize them into a few convenient but unrewarding stereotypes.

▓ Exercise 4 – My change reaction profile

To begin with, it can be useful to have an understanding of how we, as individuals, react to changes in our life – or at least to get a clearer reading of our own change reaction preference. Understanding our own reactions to change increases our capacity to deal with it. Overleaf is a questionnaire, devised by

Philip Hodson, which will help you take your own change profile. As with most questionnaires, for maximum accuracy and impact try not to put what you perceive to be the 'best' score, but the one that accurately reflects your opinion. After you have completed the questionnaire a simple scoring system will help you to take your own change reaction reading.

The Change Questionnaire

In relation to your work, please read the following 25 statements. Beside each write down a number, from 1 to 5, to quantify how strongly you agree with each remark: 1 indicates strongly disagree; 5 indicates strongly agree; 3 indicates no strong opinion in either direction.

1 A change is as good as a rest. ☐
2 These days I seem to spend more time reorganizing my job than doing it. ☐
3 Management here is pathetic – we're lions led by donkeys. ☐
4 I just take one day at a time – why cry before you get hurt? ☐
5 I'm not totally sure where the organization is going but I'm beginning to get better vibes. ☐
6 If things keep changing like this, eventually I don't think I'm going to fit in any more. ☐
7 As long as my job is safe, I don't really care what is happening. ☐
8 The best feeling at work is that sense of being stretched and learning something new. ☐
9 After all the recent changes, I'll never be afraid of change again. ☐
10 I'm always coming up with new ideas. ☐
11 I do my bit and let the rest get on with it. ☐
12 If it ain't broke, why fix it? ☐
13 Change never stops. ☐
14 There's a light at the end of the tunnel. ☐
15 After all, you can't make an omelette without breaking eggs. ☐
16 Nowadays I actually look forward to going to work. ☐
17 Every cloud has a silver lining. ☐
18 I keep my head down and my nose clean. ☐
19 I'm getting a real sense of job satisfaction. ☐

20 I feel like I'm really getting somewhere at last. ☐

21 Change is progress. ☐

22 This organization is in crisis – what's new? ☐

23 Change is usually for the better. ☐

24 Better to change than to stay still. ☐

25 It's just change for change's sake round here. ☐

I would like to thank Video Arts Ltd, who have kindly allowed me to reproduce and make changes to this questionnaire.

How to work out your score

Add together your scores as follows.

Total the scores for questions 4, 7, 11, 18 and 22:

this is your 'negation' score.

Total the scores for questions 2, 3, 6, 12 and 25:

this is your 'self-justification' score.

Total the scores for questions 5, 8, 10, 14 and 17:

this is your 'exploration' score.

Total the scores for questions 9, 15, 16, 19 and 20:

this is your 'resolution' score.

Ignore scores for questions 1, 13, 21, 23 and 24.

What do my scores tell me?

The way you interpret your scores will depend on whether you are currently in the midst of significant change in your working or non-working life.

If you are coping with change at present, your highest overall score will give an indication of the stage you have reached in coming to terms with this particular change, because it is likely to be at the forefront of your thinking.

If there are no significant changes currently taking place in your life (and this is less and less likely in the modern world), your scores will indicate whether you tend to enjoy change or find it a little more threatening. High scores in the dimensions 'exploration' and 'resolution' suggest you enjoy change. If your highest scores are in the dimensions 'negation' or 'self-justification', this suggests you that may find change a tougher ordeal.

It is important to keep this questionnaire in perspective. It is a very rough indicator and not absolute truth. I have used this exercise many times with many people from around the world, and among those who show me their questionnaires it is interesting that most have their score in each dimension in the 15–19 range with no real standout score. Perhaps this indicates, without a highly rigorous analysis, that many of us, except in the most serious of change circumstances, have all the different arguments in each dimension floating around in our head and that we move regularly across each of the dimensions as we grapple with the change until we reach acceptance and 'resolution'.

For a deeper analysis of each of the stages, refer back to the change section in Chapter 7 (page 159).

References

■ Books

I drew on the following for material relevant to this book:

Barker, Joel, *Paradigms: The Business of Discovering the Future*, Harper Business, 1993
Brown, Mark, *The Dinosaur Strain*, ICE Books, 1993
Claxton, Guy, *Noises from the Darkroom*, Aquarian, 1994
Claxton, Guy, *Hare Brain, Tortoise Mind*, Fourth Estate, 1997
Covey, Stephen R., *The Seven Habits of Highly Effective People*, Simon & Schuster, 1989
de Bono, Edward, *De Bono's Thinking Course*, BBC Books, 1994
Draaisma, Douwe, *Why Life Speeds Up As You Get Older*, Cambridge University Press, 2004
Goleman, Daniel, *Emotional Intelligence*, Bloomsbury, 1996
Goleman, Daniel, *Working with Emotional Intelligence*, Bloomsbury, 1998
Hillenbrand, Laura, *Seabiscuit: Three Men and a Racehorse*, Fourth Estate, 2001
Kane, Pat, *The Play Ethic*, Macmillan, 2004
Metcalf, C.W. and Felible, Roma, *Lighten Up*, Perseus Publishing, 1999
Miller, Douglas, *The Positive Mental Attitude Pocketbook*, Management Pocketbooks, 2005
Piaget, Jean, *Success and Understanding*, RKP, 1978
Scott, Donald, *The Psychology of Work*, RKP, 1970
Simpson, Liz, *Working from the Heart*, Vermilion, 1999
Trompenaars, Fons, and Hampden-Turner, Charles, *Riding the Waves of Culture*, Nicholas Brealey, 1994
Ventrella, Scott, *The Power of Positive Thinking in Business*, Vermilion, 2001
von Oech, Roger, *A Whack on the Side of the Head*, HarperCollins, 1990

I also mentioned the following:

Barnes, Julian, *Letters from London*, Picador, 1995
Coupland, Douglas, *Microserfs*, Flamingo, 1996
de Graaf, John et al, *Affluenza: The All-consuming Epidemic*, Berrett-Koehler, 2001
Orwell, George, *Coming Up for Air*, Penguin, 1962
Pearson, Alison, *I Don't Know How She Does It*, Vintage, 2003

■ TV/Video

Fish!, Charthouse International, featuring Pike Place Fish Market, 1998
Days of Change, Melrose, featuring leading psychotherapist Philip Hodson, 1995
www.videoarts.co.uk
Arctic Challenge, BBC Worldwide, originally broadcast in the UK 27 October 2004

Acknowledgements

Many people helped, knowingly or not, in the preparation of this book. I would like to thank Carlos Rodriguez, without whom it would not have been written. A real 'champion' – and positive thinkers need them! I am deeply grateful to have come into contact with many marvellous people who have told me more about positive thinking than all the theory in the world. There are many heroes and heroines out there, and I met some of them. So a thank you to Sergio (and to Jenny Pilling at the United Nations who 'found' him for me – a great guy!), Gavin, Kath, Helene and all the storytellers who feature in this book. Thank you to Emma Shackleton at the BBC for backing me to write it. I am deeply indebted to my text editor, Christine King, who challenged the assumptions, inaccuracies and woolly thinking in the original manuscript, and to Trish Burgess, the project editor.

On the content side I would like to thank Professor Mark Brown, who continues to allow me to take from his excellent book *The Dinosaur Strain,* and from many of the discussions that we have had over the years that he probably thought I had forgotten. Sometimes when thoughts come into your head it is hard to know if they are genuinely yours or if someone else lodged them there. There are maybe a few Mark Brown thoughts in this book that have gone unacknowledged. I must thank Chris Carling at ChrisCoach.com, who gave up much of her own time to get to grips with the original manuscript and add her expertise. The faults and inaccuracies are, of course, my own.

I would also like to record my thanks to my friends at the OSCE and UN. When I visit countries where those organizations have a presence I am reminded what positive thinking really means.

If there are a lot of baby references in the book, it is because baby Isabelle spent the first four months of her life watching her irritable father gaze at an iMac screen. As did her sister Lily and their mother Caroline. For my family I am thankful.

A final esoteric thanks to Brian Eno, Nitin Sawhney, Anouar Brahem, Miles Davis and various Brazilian musicians who provided the aural entertainment and mood creation when it was needed.

I would welcome emails from any readers who would like to contact me. My email address is: doug@dougmiller.demon.co.uk

Readers who would like to know more about Gavin's charity work can go to: www.movingmountains.org.uk